Melinda & Robert
Schoutens

FRESH AIR KIDS
SWITZERLAND

FRESH AIR
KIDS
SWITZERLAND

52 Inspiring Hikes That Will Make
Kids and Parents Happy

Melinda & Robert
Schoutens

HELVETIQ

To Noah and Tessa our two greatest teachers.

Thank you for providing the inspiration for this book and for enduring all of our family hikes. Our hope is that each kilometer spent on the trail has ignited a lifelong love of the outdoors. Whether you may have realized it or not, the time we spent outside as a family connected us to something so much greater than ourselves. May that connection guide, inspire, and propel you to be stewards of the planet.

To our parents for your guidance and wisdom, which has cultivated our desire to grasp each and every opportunity.

Mom, thank you for the imagination behind the book title and to Dad you are forever the brightest star in the sky.

To all those who supported this project from its infancy to its finish, we are indebted for your time, your enthusiasm, and your belief in us. As many of you already know, this book is far more than the pages that follow; it is a belief, a lifestyle, and a deep passion.

To our siblings, friends, and readers, may all of your journeys include rising and setting suns, some dirt, and most importantly, experiences that leave you full of wonder.

Content

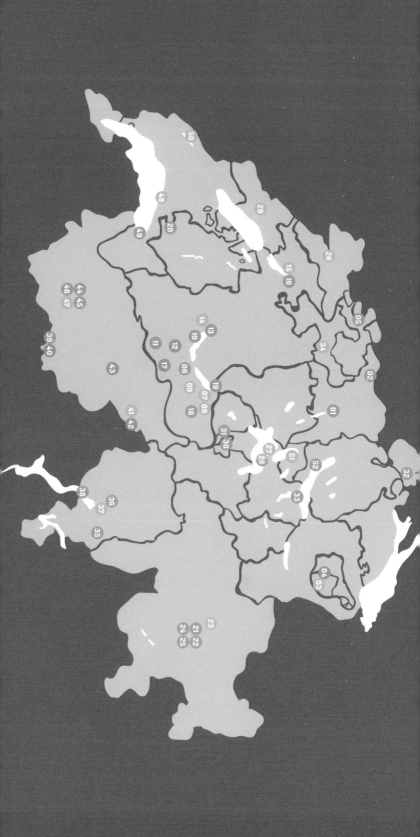

Map of Hikes

CHAPTER I

The Magic of Nature

"

Of all the paths you take in life,
make sure a few of them are dirt.

"

JOHN MUIR
NATURALIST AND AUTHOR

We tasted the sweetness of the Swiss mountains long before we ever welcomed children into our lives. The mountains ignited a love in us that was too deep to abandon and when we found ourselves expecting our first child, we vowed that we would continue to spend time outside, passing on the many gifts of the natural world. As our family continued to grow, together, we would hike, explore, and absorb all of the magic nature had to offer.

From pregnancy, to babies, to toddlers and now children, we have been outside hiking as a family for years. We have changed diapers on trails, stopped to nurse a crying baby, wrapped our children up in winter gear as we boarded gondolas and together, as a family, we have covered countless kilometers on the trails.

Throughout the years we have been met with the same sense of surprise whenever we mention our hiking excursions. Perhaps hiking appears to be an elusive pastime for some, or the drudgery of climbing steep mountains to others, but the reality is that this sport – this time spent outside – is accessible, rarely strenuous, often necessary, and available to all. Requiring little equipment, some basic knowledge, and the desire to take life out of doors, hiking can be viewed as the perfect family activity.

Our primary goal in creating *Fresh Air Kids* is to encourage families of all ages to spend more time outdoors. This book was designed to allow readers to flip through the pages and select a hike or location without all the inconvenience of having to research your day or holiday in advance, which ultimately becomes another barrier to spending quality time outside. With the guesswork eliminated, and the planning in place, we want families to pack their bags and go! We aren't promising perfect or effortless, however, we are encouraging a natural slowing down, a closeness with nature and a sense of happiness that might have otherwise never have happened.

As we spend more time outside, we enable our children to become freer in their play, creative in their mindset and inquisitive with their discoveries. We often say, "Dirt and mud are indications of a day well spent." By allowing our children to get dirty, to stick their tiny hands in the mud and become entrenched in the elements, they will experience tremendous joy and, as parents, we will too.

The health benefits of spending time outside are now coming to the forefront of books, articles, and journals. Some of the advantages of being immersed in nature include enhanced emotional well-being, increased physical vitality, and improved sleep. Being connected to the Earth is essential in today's world where individuals spend more time than ever indoors and connected to technology.

An additional benefit of exploring outdoor options for your family is that such adventures create an entirely new and diverse array of family activities to add to your repertoire. Now, when the question, "What are we going to do this weekend?" arises, the answer is simple, "Get outside."

Getting your children outside shouldn't be a chore; in fact, it should be a true pleasure. As you spend more time outside, you may notice various benefits. Nature can:

- enable a natural slowing down for both parents and children, and provide a break and a much-needed absence of technology in our lives;

- provide family time in a unique and natural setting and encourage you to become more active, exercise more frequently, and increase your physical well-being;

- allow children to connect, learn, and appreciate the natural world and encourage respect and empathy towards animals and their natural environment;

- be an educational tool to teach children about life cycles;

- heighten the senses and assist with agility, coordination, and gross motor skills;

- introduce children to critical thinking skills and be the platform to teach our children important life skills, such as reading a map and recognizing weather changes, as well as building a proper fire and extinguishing its flames;

- afford children the opportunity to play without the confines of walls and indoor rules and provide the sense of freedom they crave.

We hope families observe the power that nature and fresh air have on their children. Too often, families shy away from hiking because they believe their children are not capable of covering the distance, or fear weather that is less than perfect. Both obstacles can quickly be overcome with good planning, proper clothing, and the ability to insert joy along the way. We provide tips in chapter 2 on how to do all that!

Let us remember that when children are engaged in the world around them and absorbed in the landscape, they are often inspired to walk, play, and discover. Encourage your family to experience all of the benefits of the natural world; for us, it has made all the difference.

Melinda & Robert

CHAPTER II

Hitting the Trails

66

When children come into contact with nature they reveal their strength.

99

MARIA MONTESSORI
EDUCATOR AND PHYSICIAN

How Do You Hike with Children?

Whenever we tell people we went for a hike with our children, the response is usually the same: "How do you hike with your children?" We promise you it is possible, though we will not guarantee that it is always without complaint, multiple stops, and creative attempts at peeing or pooping in the woods, and let us not forget lots of positive reinforcement.

Switzerland is the perfect place to start hiking as a family. With its beauty, and thousands of kilometers of well-marked trails, families are certain to enjoy each hiking experience.

Despite occasional whimpers and whines, some of our happiest moments as a family were and are spent exploring. Whether hiking on local trails or in the Alps, we have listed a few tips and tricks that will help get your family out the door and into nature.

Step One
This is probably the most important step of all – *prepare yourself mentally*. Take an extra shot of patience in the morning, pat yourself on the back and know you can do this! Fresh air, dirt beneath your feet and trees all have incredible healing powers; allow the beauty of nature to wash over you and start to relax.

Step Two
To get started, *start small*. Select a hike classified as "easy" from the book. At the very least bring this book as a reference to help navigate your way.

Step Three
Try to select a trail that offers incredible scenery and *some fun,* with opportunities to play along the way. Almost all of the hikes outlined in our book offer just that (a playground, lake, stream, waterfall, animal farm, an incredible place to stay the night, etc.)! A playground at the conclusion of any trail is always a great incentive to keep children walking.

Step Four
Stop for a picnic. Pack a sheet or a blanket, your lunch and spread yourselves out. Relax, eat, drink, and enjoy the scenery that surrounds you. Breaks are essential when hiking with children, plus, who doesn't love a picnic in nature? If there is a grilling spot, be sure to pack food for grilling such as: sausages, vegetables, and bread. Teach your children the joy of making a fire, general fire safety and how to properly extinguish the flames when finished.

Step Five
Take your time and allow your children to pick up stones (though please educate your children on the importance of not throwing or kicking stones on trails for safety reasons), find the perfect walking stick, collect bugs but let them go. Search for the moon, discover shapes in the clouds; all of these little games help children discover the joy of being in nature. We also create hand drawn scavenger hunts for our chil-

dren encouraging them to find certain treasures along the trail. Please see chapter 4, which provides hands-on experiences for children of all ages.

Step Six

To avoid dips in energy, *pack plenty of snacks* and include some favorite treats. Our kids go crazy for gummy bears and sometimes that is just what we need to get us through the final stretch. But don't hand them out all at once: one here, one there, or incentivize children by saying, "When we get to the tree with the bird-house you can have another gummy bear."

Step Seven

Set a timer. If you are experiencing excessive whining – believe us, this might just happen – set a timer and encourage the group to hike for 20 minutes without stopping. As the timer rings, set another timer for 20 minutes. The later 20 minutes is for pure relaxation. Find a perfect spot to sit, eat a snack, drink water, and regroup as a team. Once your family is refreshed, continue on.

Step Eight

Recruit some friends. Nothing takes little minds off the kilometers they will cover like having a good friend to walk with, but make sure their friend is accustomed to walking and enjoys nature as much as your children do!

Step Nine

Make it fun! *Pick a theme* for your hike, such as spring flowers, and make it your job as nature detectives to find and identify as many as you can. If you are worried about running out of ideas, don't worry; there are plenty of ideas for keeping children occupied in chapter 4.

Step Ten

Find your family's *"sweet spot."* The "sweet spot" is the length of a hike a family will take pleasure in with the least amount of whining and effort. Though it is not always easy to determine this, once you do, try your best to stick to that amount or less for more pleasant hikes. Prior to starting out on the excursion, assess the mood and energy levels of the family. If energy is low, opt for a shorter or easier hike.

Step Eleven

If your children are little, please bring along an easy-to-pack, soft-sided *carrier.* There is nothing worse than having to carry a tired child without the assistance of a carrier. For safety purposes, it is essential to have your hands free while hiking.

Step Twelve

Just go! If your children are actively engaged at home playing a game and you ask them if they are up for a hike, the answer will more than likely be a loud and boisterous "No!" Understandable. But sharing nature as a family provides precious and invaluable time together, and the games will still be there upon your return.

Step Thirteen

If you need one more reason or tip to get you started, consider this: as humans *we crave and need the natural world.* More than ever, we require the grounding opportunities that only nature can provide. This subject is now coming to the forefront in academic research.

Step Fourteen
Be flexible and *maintain your sense of humor*. There are days on the trail that are just tough and no amount of planning can avoid difficult times. Remain calm, try to play a game or make a joke, and if nothing works, head home.

Gentle Steps

Switzerland has unprecedented beauty and it is our responsibility to maintain and protect its natural landscape because, let's be honest, there is a lot to protect here. Whenever we are in nature, it is our duty as parents, caretakers, and/or guardians, to model respect for the environment, the land, and our surroundings. Remember you are the teacher, so teach and guide well.

When in nature, be sure to be aware of the following:

Risks
Whenever in the mountains it is important to remember to enter such environments with deep regard. The mountains and all that surrounds them are extremely powerful, and venturing into nature has inherent risks. Always be aware of falling rocks, avalanches, and changing weather conditions. If you have questions, members of the hotel staff or local Tourist Information Centers are typically good resources to consult, as are chairlift and gondola operators.

Weather
Conditions can change quickly in the mountains. Never attempt alpine hikes in poor weather. It is essential to check weather forecasts before starting out on any hike.

Comfort Level
Whenever in doubt regarding the safety of a trail, trust your gut and walk away. It is better to appreciate the beauty of an area from afar, rather than enter into a situation that may be unsafe.

Trails

Stay on the trails. They are designated walking zones. By leaving the trail, you risk becoming lost or injured, or causing harm to others, the environment, and natural habitats.

Animals

Do not feed animals, or get too close to them. If you come across cows, be aware that these animals may be extremely protective of their young. Use caution when walking near calves and provide them with ample space.

Fences

You should always close fences and gates whenever passing through farms, pastures, and open fields.

Grilling

Whenever cooking with an open fire, be sure to do so safely. Please put out a fire before departing a particular site. In addition, heed the advice of posted signs. If the year has been particularly dry, warnings may appear that it is not suitable to create a fire.

Trash

Throw garbage away (apple cores, snack wrappers, lunch remains, etc.) in designated trash bins. If there are no trash bins available, pack out your trash and carry it with you. Please do not spit chewing gum out on the trail.

Dogs

If you have a dog, be sure to clean up after the animal and keep it on a leash wherever posted.

Flowers

Do not allow your children to pick any flowers. They will wilt before you get back home and some may be protected.

Stinging Nettle – Ouch!

Stinging nettles are abundant on the trails. If you or your children touch a stinging nettle, know that the antidote plant, dock weed, typically grows in close proximity. Pick a leaf of dock weed, crush the leaf in your hands and rub it on the stinging area to minimize the pain. If you are unable to find dock weed, wash the area with cool water and try not to scratch your skin. Once you have access to soap, wash the area gently and place (by dabbing) a paste of baking soda and water on the affected area. Anti-itch cream can help too.

Understanding Trail Markers

Yellow: Hiking Trails

The majority of the hikes outlined in this book are on yellow hiking routes. The yellow hiking paths are typically wide, but not always. These trails are the safest for families hiking with children. This is not to say they may not require special attention to inherent risks, however. It is always advised to wear hiking boots with good tread, and not sneakers, when hiking.

White–Red–White: Mountain Trails

The Mountain Trails may be steep, narrow in some areas, and may include sharp drops or edges. Individuals hiking on these trails should be comfortable with their hiking abilities, wearing good hiking shoes and be wary of potential rock falls and steep ascents and descents.

White–Blue–White: Alpine Trails

Of all the trails, the Alpine Trails are those that often require a high level of hiking experience and mountaineering skills. Such trails may be at higher altitudes, over scree (loose stones), glaciers, and rock with the potential need to use ropes, crampons, and other hiking equipment. These trails may not be suitable for children and best left for those who are comfortable taking risks.

Pink: Winter Hiking Trails

These trails are designated as winter hiking paths for walking, snowshoeing, and sledding.

Theme Trails

Some trails are labeled "Theme Trails," and thus have their own trail markers either named after the particular theme trail or indicated by an icon or a picture.

Yellow-Red Border Sign

The half yellow, half red border signs advise individuals of a wildlife-protected area. These border signs are posted to direct hikers not to enter these areas.

Languages Used on Trail Markers

In each region, the trail markers will be labeled according to the local language. Be aware that this will vary according to the different locations within Switzerland.

Trail Maintenance, Trail Closures, and Changes to Trails

It is quite possible that some of the trails mentioned in this book are either under maintenance, closed due to weather conditions, or have changed over the course of time. We have done our best to provide accurate information in this book. We apologize if the information provided is not correct and would like to hear from you should this be the case (info@helvetiq.ch). To determine if the route you have selected is currently open and safe for hiking, it is advisable to contact one of the following resources before starting your journey:

- Local Tourist Information Centers
  (may show trail status for summer and winter activities)

- *www.myswitzerland.com*

- The Swiss Hiking Trail Federation – *www.wandern.ch* (DE) /
  www.randonner.ch (FR)

- The Swiss Alpine Club – *www.sac-cas.ch*

How to Read Trail Markers

- The center of the trail markers, or the white section, lists your current position and elevation. The white middle section may not be present on all trail signs.

- Each town name or waypoint indicates the destination along with the estimated time it will take to reach that location from your current position without stopping. For example, "Arlesheim 1 h 30 min" means Arlesheim can be reached in roughly 1.5 hours. Always allow extra time to reach the final destination when hiking with children. Our general rule is to double the indicated time on the trail marker, to allow for stops, refueling along the way and ample playtime.

- The names on the trail markers of destinations often include icons for a train, tram, bus, boat and/or gondola stations. Those icons indicate that a specific mode of transportation is available at the end point. On occasion, the icon may be for a viewpoint, picnic spot, Tourist Information Center, or restaurant.

- Some trail markers may not contain names. However, they may display a route logo or color codes. Such markers may indicate regional and local highlighted routes or theme trails.

- The yellow diamonds (with a person hiking, plain yellow, with words, canton emblem, etc.), as well as the white-red-white painted lines and white-blue-white painted lines along the trails are confirmation that you are on the route.

- Trail markers may appear on trees, rocks, buildings, trashcans, poles, fences, or other objects along the route. Look for the trail markers as you hike to ensure you are on the correct route.

We have done our best to provide accurate directions and maps of each route outlined in this book. Our hope is that the directions serve as a reference and are not your only guide while hiking.

How To Use This Book

Trail Difficulty

We categorize all hikes in this book as easy, moderate, or challenging.

Easy
These hikes or walks indicate that participants can enjoy this route with minimum effort. The trails are relatively easy for children to navigate. The hike is not particularly long in distance and may be, though not always, stroller-friendly, which we will indicate accordingly. Easy hikes are the ideal place for beginners to start.

Moderate
These hikes signify that the trail may be long in length, may require some uphill climbs or steep descents. They are certainly manageable for most individuals with some hiking experience. Moderate hikes are great for individuals or families that are comfortable hiking and have spent some time outdoors.

Challenging
These hikes deserve more time and more trail awareness. They may have steep ascents and descents or ridgelines, requiring a bit more skill, concentration, and general knowledge. Challenging hikes are not recommended for first-time hikers. These hikes are best left for those with experience and parents that are comfortable assisting their children whenever necessary. Harnesses are often recommended for children on such routes. Hiking poles may also be useful.

Distance and Length of Hikes

We have done our best to accurately indicate the distance and time of each hike listed in the book. Please take all lengths and times as reasonable estimates. Be aware that GPS tracking and smartphone apps are valuable tools, however, from our experience the positional accuracy and length of each route can vary significantly due to multiple factors.

Types of Hikes

Loop
Starts and finishes in the same location taking you in a circular route.

Out–and–back
Route that returns you along the same path you hiked out on.

Point–to–point
The start point is different from the end point.

Transportation

Car-free
All of the hikes outlined in this book have been completed by us and are with very few exceptions accessible with public transportation. If driving, know that most hikes start from a public transportation stop, a gondola, funicular, etc.

Start/End Point
We have listed each start/end point as shown on the *SBB.ch* website. We indicate if the stop is a train, bus, etc. in parenthesis for each hike if this information is not explicit. On occasion a start or end point will not be a transportation site, but a hotel, lake, or other destination, which is clearly indicated. Some locations are accessible by foot only, in which case an overnight stay is recommended.

Buses
Hikes that rely on a bus for transportation may not be the best option on Sundays or holidays due to the infrequency in which they run. Plan accordingly by viewing timetables before your hike.

Pictograms

Whenever you see a pictogram within chapter 3, the hike will include one or more of the special features listed below.

 Animals (zoo, farm)

 High mountains

 Flowers

 Ice cream/Treats

 Lake

 Theme trail

 Boat rental/ Boat trip

 Toboggan run

 Castle

 Playground

 Waterfall

 Cave

 Ruin/Bunker

Safety First

Hiking has inherent risks that must be assumed by all participants. Every individual is responsible for his or her own safety, and the safety of their children while on trails, near bodies of water, and whenever in nature. Be responsible, smart, and safe.

Children are undoubtedly easier to manage and keep track of the smaller they are, but as they grow and learn to hike more independently, it is important that they are educated on the importance of staying on the trail and reading trail markers, as well as learning how to prevent falls and signal for help. Children should always stay within sight of adults, or the trail leader whenever hiking. When crossing over dangerous or risky areas with children, either harness the child, or keep the child on the inside of the trail. As children grow older, they should learn to carry their own backpack with water, snacks, a light jacket, a small first-aid kit, and a whistle for safety purposes. If a child becomes lost on a trail, he or she should stay where they are and use the whistle to signal for help. By educating our children on safety prior to starting out on hikes, we provide them with the knowledge and skills they require to hike with confidence.

Whenever hiking on unfamiliar trails, especially at higher elevations, it is advised to pack a harness or a rope for your child(ren). Despite the looks you may encounter, it is better to be safe than regretful. Know how to safely use a rope prior to hiking. We assume no responsibility for individuals who read this book and participate in hikes outlined on the pages that follow.

In case of an emergency please remember the Rega Emergency Number 1414.

Equipment Check

What to Wear

Whenever hiking, be sure to wear comfortable, outdoor clothing. Hiking pants that dry quickly and zip off to become shorts are ideal, as are functional T-shirts and long sleeves. During the height of tick season, it is advised to wear long sleeves and pants in light colors. Individuals with long hair should keep their hair back and in a hat.

It is strongly advised to always wear proper hiking boots with good tread. Please know that sneakers or tennis shoes are not a substitute for hiking boots. Hiking socks are advisable and make a difference when it comes to general comfort.

What to Pack

We typically carry one or two backpacks for day trips. Our children pack and carry their own small backpacks, but we carry the majority of the load on longer journeys. All of the supplies listed below should easily fit into a 30-liter backpack.

Hats

Sun hats or baseball caps are ideal to shield your face and eyes from the sun's intense rays, and winter hats offer protection from cold temperatures by providing an extra layer of warmth.

Sunglasses

Bring a pair of sunglasses for everyone in your group, especially if you plan to hike in winter and summer when the sun can be particularly intense and can reflect off water and/or snow.

Scarves and Bandanas

These items can serve multiple purposes and come in handy in both hot and cold weather. On hot days, dip the bandana in water and wrap around your head or neck to instantly cool the body. Scarves or bandanas can also be used as small towels to dry wet bodies or to provide warmth.

Weatherproof Clothes

As seasons change, but always when hiking in the Alps, be prepared for all types of weather. It can change without warning. Pack an extra layer of warm clothing. Durable jackets, such as, fleece, or down and/or rain jackets that can easily be folded up, requiring very little space, are ideal for hiking. Also, consider rain pants if the forecast indicates rain. A small pair of gloves or mittens helps to keep hands warm when the temperatures fall and can be stored easily.

A Change of Clothes

Be sure to have a spare change of clothes, which is essential for children of all ages when participating in long hikes. Typically a T-shirt, clean underwear, socks and lightweight pants will do the trick. If you have children close in age, pack one set of the older child's clothes that either child can wear if necessary to save space.

Sandals or Flip-flops

Though this might seem like a luxury item, we can assure you there is nothing more enjoyable than slipping your feet into sandals after being locked up in socks and boots all day. Throw sandals into your bag and relish the fresh air on your toes. Don't forget to pack a small foldable bag to place your hiking boots and socks in.

Hiking Poles

Some people require the extra stability that poles provide when hiking. Pack poles for long treks, or for hikes that require a great deal of ascents and descents.

Plenty of Water

Water is essential for every hike, so either invest in a large hydration pack (water bladder) or a few quality water bottles that are sturdy and built to last. Be sure each member of your family has his or her own bottle of water that holds enough water for each journey. Never rely on water being available along the trails. When hiking in the winter months, we recommend packing hot tea, coffee, or hot chocolate for the group, which is a great way to warm-up along the trail.

Food

Pack plenty of food for each hike. Ideal food for walks includes: fruit (fresh and dried), vegetables, trail mix, hard-boiled eggs, crackers, cheese, sandwiches, sausages, and pizza dough (aka Schlangenbrot, which is wrapped around a stick for grilling) if you plan to grill or picnic. Consider packing a thin picnic blanket.

Treats

Having a special treat for your group can be the extra incentive you need to get your little ones through the last leg of what may be a long hike.

Plastic Bags

Plastic bags are very helpful. Old coffee bags that once housed whole bean or ground coffee are great for carrying stinky trash, as they do an incredible job of masking nasty odors. Remember that the planet doesn't need more plastic waste, so do your best to use only what you need and dispose of waste properly.

Wet Wipes and Diapers

Wet wipes serve multiple purposes. Pack plenty. If necessary, take diapers with you.

Sunscreen

Trails are often exposed. Because this means little to no shade, which leaves the skin vulnerable and subject to burns, be sure to pack plenty of sunscreen.

Knife

We cannot emphasize enough how often we use our multi-purpose, Swiss Army knives when we hike. We cut fruit, remove splinters with the tweezers, saw wood, etc. If you do not have a multi-purpose knife, consider purchasing one. Pack a small knife for children as well. With proper instruction and supervision, children will enjoy time whittling sticks.

Matches/Lighter/Newspaper

If you plan to grill while hiking, pack matches or a lighter, plus a bit of newspaper to get your fire started.

Soft-Sided Carrier

A soft-sided carrier is a frameless backpack that is ideal for small children. These carriers pack easily and provide a refuge for tired feet and weary bodies.

Harnesses or Rope for Safety

We purchased a harness at a local store and always carry it with us whenever we are in a new hiking area or are unfamiliar with a particular trail. Our children do not like to wear their harnesses; however, our first priority as parents is their safety.

Stroller

Whenever we refer to strollers in this book, we are referring to large, three-wheeled sport or all terrain strollers. Please do not attempt to hike with umbrella strollers or street strollers. Not only will your hike be miserable with your inability to push your child, but you may also be placing your child in danger. Whenever we hiked with a stroller, we used an arm tether and tightly wrapped it around our wrist for safety.

Phone/Camera

Do not forget to bring your phone or even your camera. There is nothing more enjoyable than capturing the tranquility of the trails and your children in nature. You will reflect on these images for years to come. A cell phone may also be used as a safety tool should you be able to receive cell service while on the trails.

Wallet

Bring your travel passes (tram, train, Half Fare Travel Card, Junior Travelcard, etc.), health insurance cards, your ID card, permit or photo identification when crossing borders as well as other discount cards (e. g. Museum Pass). In terms of money, it is advisable to take cash with you and make sure to always have some change in your wallet.

Half Fare Travel Card (Halbtax)

The SBB Half Fare train ticket is a phenomenal deal and worth the investment if you frequent trains throughout the year. This card, offering discounted train fare across Switzerland, costs under CHF 200 per year.

Junior Travelcard

The SBB Junior Travelcard is for children six-years of age and older when traveling with a parent. At a cost of just CHF 30 per year, children travel free of charge from six until their sixteenth birthday on most forms of transportation (within the half-fare travel zones) as long as the child is accompanied by his or her parent. To determine where the Junior Travelcard is valid, simply visit the SBB website and download the "Synoptic Map."

Medical Kit

Never leave home without having an adequately stocked first-aid kit:

+ Pain reliever for both adults and children
+ Adhesive bandages in an array of sizes
+ Antiseptic spray
+ Insect repellent, especially for ticks – we prefer natural blends, which are available at a local drug store
+ Cream to help with insect bites and stings
+ Arnica cream for bruises
+ Arnica tablets
+ Gauze
+ Saline
+ Stomach medication

Helpful Resources

Myswitzerland.com

Myswitzerland.com is a tremendous online resource, created by the National Tourist Information Organization. The site provides inspiration for numerous activities and locations throughout Switzerland. Detailed information on Switzerland's geography, customs, and history is also available on the site.

SwitzerlandMobility App

This free app provides detailed maps of Switzerland with over 60,000 km of hiking routes within the country. Winter and summer activities, transportation stops, points of interest, a compass, and GPS are also included. For more information on this app and the services provided, visit the website: *www.schweizmobil.ch*

SBB Mobile App

The SBB Mobile travel app is simple, user-friendly, and allows for ticket purchases, provides timetables and schedule changes as well as general information. For more information on this app and the services provided, visit the website: *www.sbb.ch*

Bergfex Touren App

This free app is used to track and retain outdoor recreation. It provides topographical maps in Europe, allowing users to track and record outdoor activities, such as hiking, biking, running, etc. For more information on this app and the services provided, visit the website: *www.bergfex.com*

Rega App

Download the Rega emergency app, which can be used within Switzerland and just beyond the Swiss borders. This app is available for free and can be used should an emergency occur while hiking in the mountains. For more information on this app and the services provided, visit the website: *www.rega.ch*

MeteoSwiss App

For weather in Switzerland, download the MeteoSwiss App. For more information on this app and the services provided, visit the website: *www.meteoschweiz.admin.ch*

Download the Hikes

For more information about the hiking routes, download the GPX files from the Helvetiq website *(www.helvetiq.com)* prior to starting your adventure. GPX files can be uploaded to most hiking apps; we recommend *bergfex.com* where GPX files can be added to your "Tours."

The Backpack Checklist

- ○ This book or directions that include access to transportation timetables
- ○ Hats for sun and warmth
- ○ Sunglasses
- ○ Rain gear/Warm clothes
- ○ Scarves/Gloves
- ○ A change of clothes for children
- ○ Hiking poles
- ○ Water
- ○ Food/Treats
- ○ Wet Wipes
- ○ Diapers
- ○ Plastic bags
- ○ Medical kit
- ○ Sunscreen
- ○ Swiss Army Knife
- ○ Matches
- ○ Soft-sided carrier
- ○ Harness or rope for safety
- ○ Stroller
- ○ Phone/Camera
- ○ Wallet with all the essentials

_____

_____

The Minimalists' Pack

Go light, go easy, but go prepared.

- O Medical kit
- O Water
- O Food/Treats
- O Cell phone
- O Wallet with all the essentials
- O Change of clothes
- O Fleece jacket

The Weekend Pack

Go heavier, but go ready to enjoy a few days away by adding the following items to the "Backpack Checklist" for everyone in your group.

- O Toothbrush, toothpaste, deodorant, shampoo, soap (some hotels or mountain houses provide these, but always pack a toothbrush)
- O Pajamas
- O Flip-flops
- O Fleece jacket
- O Change of clothes

Backpack Tip

Interested in hiking without all the preparation? Always leave a family backpack filled with the essentials. When you are ready to hit the trails, just grab water, snacks, and don't forget the kids!

Now all that is left to do is hit the trails!

CHAPTER III

The Hikes

Teaching children about the natural world should be treated as one of the most important events in their lives.

THOMAS BERRY
AUTHOR AND TEACHER

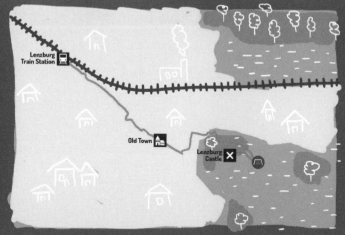

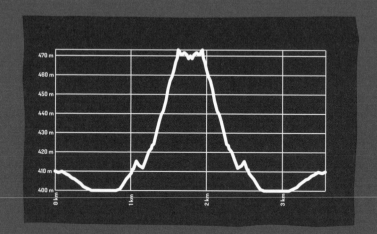

/ᒥᒥ\ **playground**

Lenzburg Castle

 01

Lenzburg, Bahnhof
(train station)

▷···

Lenzburg, Bahnhof
(train station)

···✗

1 h 15 min
(not including time spent at the castle)

3.7 km

End of March through end of October

Overview

The easy walk from the Lenzburg train station to the Lenzburg Castle is a genuine delight. Once onsite at the castle, families will immediately be captivated by the thrilling opportunities that will encourage everyone to explore. From cabins to discover, keys to be found, swords and crowns to be made, plus museums to learn from, this location is worthy of an entire day. The easy return walk to the train station can be passed quickly by reminiscing about the day's activities and the memories that were made.

Directions

Exit the Lenzburg train station and turn left towards the town continuing along Bahnhofstrasse towards "Altstadt." After approximately 0.6 km, the path turns right for a short distance, then left and continues through an underpass. After 60 m, the path will quickly turn left and then right, continuing along Bahnhofstrasse, which becomes closed to traffic before entering a lancet-arched gate into the old town. Through this gate, we recommend meandering through the few streets of the old town before continuing to the end of Rathausgasse, turning left onto Leuengasse and out of the old town. Turn left onto Kronenplatz, walking along the stone wall, and then right onto Steinbrüchliweg following the yellow trail markers which will lead up through a field to the Lenzburg Castle. Return to the train station by reversing the directions to get to the castle.

Trail Markers

Lenzburg ≫ Schloss Lenzburg ≫ Lenzburg

Tip

Entrance to the Lenzburg Castle is free with the Museum Pass, so be sure to bring the pass with you for your excursion. To find out more about the Museum Pass, which provides access to more than 300 museums in three countries (France, Germany, and Switzerland), visit the website at: *www.museumspass.com*

Special Features

+ Toilets are available at the castle.
+ There is a small play area located just before the castle walls.
+ The top floor of the castle encourages children to play, dress up, be creative, and use their wild imaginations.
+ The craft room is accessible for children to create their own swords, crowns, and an array of other items.
+ Pack a picnic lunch and enjoy the impressive grounds of the castle.
+ The castle is full of fun and engaging opportunities for children of all ages.

Be Aware

✚ This is a stroller-friendly walk but there are some steps to navigate.
✚ The museum is open from Tuesday – Sunday and on most public holidays from 10:00 – 17:00 from the end of March through the end of October. Always check the website before starting your journey: *www.schloss-lenzburg.ch*

Small Farm

Frick
Train Station

picnic   toilets

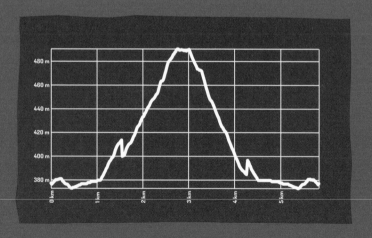

Frick Cherry Hike "Fricktaler Chriesiwäg"

Frick, Bahnhof
(train station)

Frick, Bahnhof
(train station)

---

2 h
(Kurzroute; short route)

5.8 km
(Kurzroute; short route)

Year round

However, the best time to experience this hike is in April when the cherry blossoms are in full bloom. Please note the season is short, ranging from eight to eighteen days, but it truly is gorgeous.

Overview

This hike is a visual wonder and highly anticipated during the cherry blossom season. With the white and pink buds against a vibrant green backdrop, the area is a feast for the eyes. The hike is best enjoyed during the spring to capture the cherry blossoms in all their glory.

Directions

From the train station, turn right, following the brown signs for the "Fricktaler Chriesiwäg" which is represented by a cartoon drawing of a family of cherries. The trail follows the yellow trail markers and continues to display "Fricktaler Chriesiwäg." These brown "Fricktaler Chriesiwäg" signs may appear as green arrows on poles leading the way, and will deviate from the yellow trail by directing you up Märtenweg and past a small farm. This trail will follow the road and gravel path up and around some orchards, before cresting at a grilling and picnic area with pleasant views. The trail splits at the grilling station for the Kurzroute (short route), highlighted in this book, or the Zusatzroute (alternate route). Turn left for the short route. The last section of the hike is along Landstrasse, the main street through Gipf-Oberfrick leading back to the train station.

Trail Markers

Frick Bahnhof >> Fricktaler Chriesiwäg >> Frick Bahnhof

Tip

Look for fossils! The area of Frick is known to have fossils. During this hike, we were able to find some in a modest rock pile on the trail. Take the time to dig and search; you never know what you might discover!

Special Features

+ There is a small farm not far from the start of the walk.
+ According to the website (*www.aargautourismus.ch*), cherries may be eaten when in season.
+ There is a grill pit approximately 3 km into the hike with picnic tables, a toilet, and wood.

Be Aware

+ The path is mostly paved and the short route (Kurzroute) is stroller-friendly.
+ Once walkers exit the train station, there is a short portion of the hike that is close to the road, but with sidewalk accessibility.

+ During the summer months, the trail offers little to no shade. It is therefore recommended to wear sun-hats, sunscreen, and sunglasses.

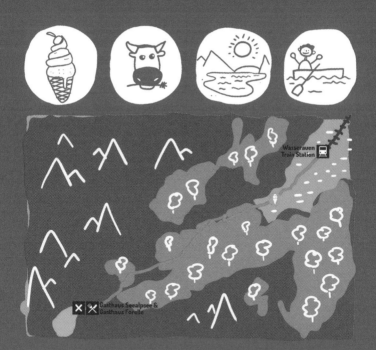

Wasserauen Train Station

Gasthaus Seealpsee & Gasthaus Forelle

 ice cream

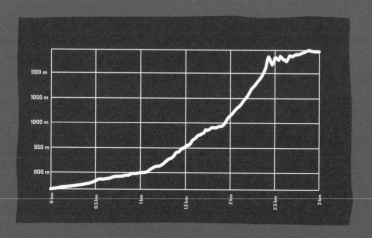

Wasserauen to Seealpsee

Wasserauen, Station
(train station)

Seealpsee
(this is not a public transportation stop)

1.5–2 h

3 km

Spring through fall
Confirm that the area is open in the spring,
as it is very seasonal and weather-dependent.

Overview

The essence of this hike is obvious upon your arrival at Seealpsee. On a clear day, the lake shines, the mountains in the distance reflect in the water, and families will enjoy a relaxing day in a perfectly natural setting.

This hike takes you up a wide, paved path, ultimately leading to picturesque Lake Seealpsee, which is only accessible by foot. The well-paved route is ideal for families with smaller children. This tranquil area is captivating and children will relish the opportunity to walk the shores of Seealpsee, splash in the water, and feel dwarfed in the grand scale of the surrounding mountains. Perfect in the spring, summer, and fall months, this area is very special.

Directions

This hike starts at the Wasserauen train station parking lot. Follow the signs to Seealpsee bearing in mind that there are two separate trails. Continue straight past the Hotel Alpenrose, at which point the path will divide in two. Continue on the paved trail and veer right over the bridge. At one point the trail marker will lead you onto a gravel path; we recommend continuing along the paved route as the gravel path will merge soon after with the road. Either way, you will end up at Seealpsee. To return to Wasserauen, follow the paved path back down.

Trail Markers

Wasserauen ›› Seealpsee

Tip

There is a small kiosk on the way up from Wasserauen, approximately 0.8 km into the hike, offering cheese, meat, and an incredibly entertaining (automatic) ice cream machine. Trust us, the kids will love the ice cream machine, so bring some change.

Special Features

+ Ideal opportunities for photographers on clear days.
+ Plenty of nature to captivate children including fish, frogs, marmots, ducks and, on occasion, ibex.
+ Easy walks available around the lake.
+ Incredible views of the Säntis and Altman.
+ Seealpsee offers swimming and boating (available for rent at guesthouse Forelle).
+ Overnights possible, and recommended, at the mountain guesthouses Seealpsee and Forelle (book in advance).

+ Side trips are possible up to Aescher by foot, or Ebenalp via the cable car from Wasserauen.

Be Aware

+ This is a White-Red-White trail.
+ We saw people with strollers on the paved path; but it is one serious uphill climb and one precarious downhill hike.
+ The paved path to Seealpsee is steep, listed as 1 h 10 minutes. Once again, allow for more time with small children.
+ There is no opportunity to fill water bottles until walkers arrive at the lake.
+ Bathrooms and food are available at guesthouses Seealpsee and Forelle.
+ Start this hike early in the day to allow for plenty of time to complete the hike and enjoy the lake's ambiance.
+ Bring a change of clothes in the event children want to swim or get wet in the lake.

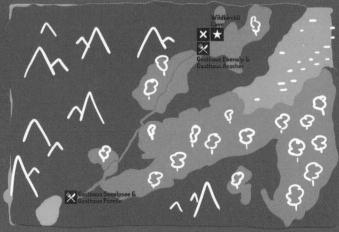

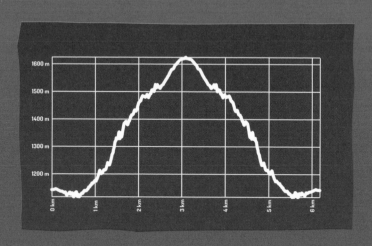

Seealpsee – Aescher – Seealpsee

Seealpsee
(this is not a public transportation stop)

Seealpsee
(this is not a public transportation stop)

3 h
(allow for more time to eat and enjoy Aescher, the Wildkirchli cave, and the paragliders at Ebenalp)

6.4 km

Spring through fall
Confirm that the area is open in the spring, as it is very seasonal and weather-dependent.

Overview

This hike is best suited for those families staying overnight at Seealpsee. This difficult, yet rewarding hike is particularly beautiful in the spring months, when the snow has melted and the spring flowers decorate the landscape. This hike offers incredible views throughout, though requires genuine effort and concentration. Once at guesthouse Aescher, take the time to relish in your hard work by enjoying a bite to eat. Allow your children to take pleasure in the resident ponies, and explore the prehistoric Wildkirchli cave (mind your step, however, as there is minimal lighting). On the hike down to Seealpsee from Aescher, it is advised to harness children for safety purposes, as there are sharp drops, though there are some cables along the route offering more stability.

Directions

From Seealpsee, head in the direction of Wasserauen. Just after a rocky overhang and cattle grate, the trail to Aescher will veer left up the hill and through fields. The trail leads into the woods and begins a series of switchbacks which deposit you into another field that slopes on one side. Another wooded section yields more switchbacks, some of which are on rocky sections although most provide cable handholds or railings. When the trail emerges from the trees, you will see Berghaus Aescher in the distance tucked under a rocky overhang. We recommend continuing up the trail to Wildkirchli Altarhöhle, a chapel tucked into a shallow cave, then further up the trail, through the Wildkirchli cave, and up to the Ebenalp lift-station to watch the paragliders take off. Further up is Berggasthaus Ebenalp which has commanding views of Seealpsee. Return to Seealpsee the way you came, but first enjoy something to eat at Ebenalp or Aescher.

Trail Markers

Seealpsee >> Aescher >> Seealpsee

Tip

The Rösti and homemade cakes at Aescher are not to be missed. For those parents not inclined to hike all the way up to Aescher, a gondola is available in Wasserauen that takes you up to Ebenalp. From Ebenalp it is just a short walk to Aescher.

Special Features

+ Gorgeous alpine flowers during the spring and summer months.
+ Incredible views.
+ The opportunity to enjoy the famous Aescher guesthouse (literally built into the mountain) including: the ambiance, the food, and their animals.

+ A walk through the Wildkirchli caves.
+ Walking up to Ebenalp, hikers may witness paragliders taking off from the mountain just below Berggasthaus Ebenalp.

Be Aware

+ This is not a stroller-friendly hike.
+ This hike includes a steep ascent and a steep descent.
+ This hike is only advised for those families accustomed to hiking on White-Red-White trails and comfortable with their hiking skills.
+ A harness is advised for children for safety.
+ This hike is not recommended in rain or poor weather due to rockslides, slick trail conditions, and overall safety.
+ All of the mountain huts are only open seasonally (typically early May through late October). Check the websites for opening times and weather conditions.

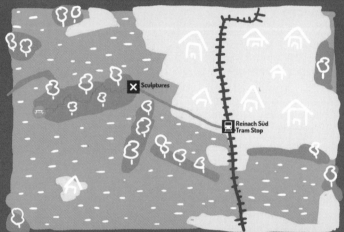

Sculptures

Reinach Süd
Tram Stop

picnic/grill spot

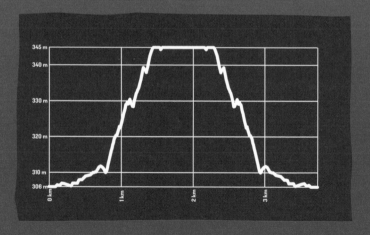

Sculpture Trail

Reinach Süd
(tram stop)

Reinach Süd
(tram stop)

1 h
(though please allow for more time as children play and explore the area)

3.7 km

Year round

Overview

Hidden among the trees in a tiny forest known as Leywald, sits a small oasis for children. With over 40 wooden sculptures (think storybook characters) and an incredible ball run, this walk will be a true pleasure for everyone.

A gigantic bench waits at the end of the hike, which will keep children occupied as adults prepare lunch at one of the grilling areas with their well-stocked wood supply.

This little trail, rich with activities, makes for an ideal, captivating and easy family adventure.

Directions

From the Basel SBB train station, tram 11 in the direction of Reinach takes you to this walk. The tram stop is Reinach Süd: follow the sign to "Waldlehrpfad Skulpturenweg," a brown sign overhead towards the back end of the tram. Proceed along Fiechtenweg (unfortunately not marked) which meanders and becomes Schützenstrasse. The road narrows and you will see a wooden sign for the "Skulpturenweg." After a 10–15-minute walk through a residential area and past a small farm building on your right, the trail starts across from the dog park indicated by the wooden "Skulturenweg" sign. This sculpture path is easy to follow and ends in a picnic and grilling area. Follow the path in reverse to return to the tram stop.

Tip

If your plan is to barbecue at the end of the trail, arrive early to secure one of the grills.

Special Features

+ This is a stroller-friendly hike.
+ Grills and ample wood are available.
+ Engaging sculpture trail.
+ This theme trail is the ideal family activity for children of all ages.

Be Aware

+ There are no water stations.
+ There are no restroom facilities.

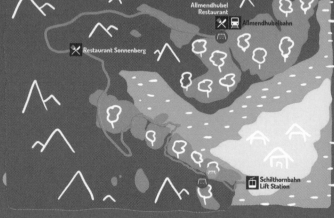

Allmendhubel
Restaurant

Allmendhubelbahn

Restaurant Sonnenberg

Schilthornbahn
Lift Station

 playground   picnic/grill spot

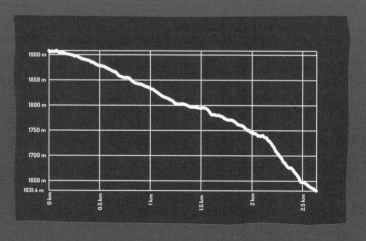

The Children's Adventure Trail

Mürren
(Allmendhubelbahn)

Mürren
(Schilthornbahn)

1 h

2.6 km

Summer through fall

Overview

The car-free village of Mürren is small, but certainly has a lively charm. Families will marvel at the scenic landscape and will have plenty of hikes and a large playground to occupy their time. Mürren is a wonderful little alpine village for hiking, playing, and simply taking in the incredible views.

The Children's Adventure Trail starts off at the Flower Park at Allmendhubel, and weaves through picturesque meadows while including a playground, which affords the children in your group the opportunity to play and have a grand time in nature.

Directions

From the top of the Allmendhubelbahn, exit the station. To the right is the Panorama Restaurant Allmendhubel and in front of the station is a large playground, both of which are great places to relax before the hike back down to Mürren.

The hike begins at the Flower Park and follows the orange trail markers labeled "Children's Adventure Trail" to the left when looking at the playground.

Once at Blumental 1841 m continue following the orange trail markers to the right. You will also see the yellow trail markers for Mürren indicating both 30 minutes and 40 minutes. Follow both the orange trail markers labeled "Children's Adventure Trail" and the trail markers down to Mürren, which is your ultimate destination.

The trail will then lead down a relatively straight descent towards the Mürren (Schilthornbahn) lift station. At the bottom of this descent, the trail will continue along a road which can be taken back to the center of Mürren or, if you're not planning to return to Mürren, you can take the lift down to the Stechelberg, Schilthornbahn lift station, which offers bus connections to your destination of choice.

Trail Markers

Allmendhubel ≫ Children's Adventure Trail ≫ Mürren

Tip

If time permits, we recommend a visit to the small and sleepy town of Gimmelwald. With just around 130 residents, the town is quaint and extremely picturesque. Upon arrival in Gimmelwald (a 35-minute walk from Mürren, though allow extra time with children) you might just stop and ask yourself if the town is real, but let us assure you, it certainly is. With a few small, but charming hotels and hostels and a wonderful patio to enjoy some delicious food served up by Pension Gimmelwald, the town is so engaging that you might just want to stay awhile, basking in the views of this storybook village.

Special Features

+ The incredible Flower Park at Allmendhubel with its alpine views.
+ Great for active children with a slide along the trail and a second playground along the route.
+ Grilling option.
+ Food and toilets are available at the Panorama Restaurant Allmendhubel.
+ There are several theme trails in this area including: The Flower Trail, which is roughly 20 min, the Northface Trail, which is longer at 2 h 30 min, and the Mountain View Trail which is 2 h. Before venturing out on new trails, check with locals and/or hotel staff to determine if the trail is child-friendly.

Be Aware

+ The Children's Adventure Trail is not stroller-friendly. Please do not even attempt to bring a stroller on this hike, rather, take a soft-sided carrier with you for when your little one grows weary.

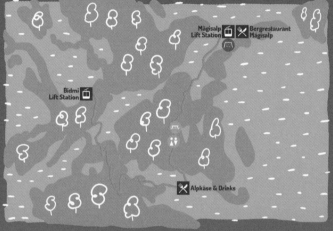

Mägisalp
Lift Station

Bergrestaurant
Mägisalp

Bidmi
Lift Station

Alpkäse & Drinks

picnic   toilets   playground

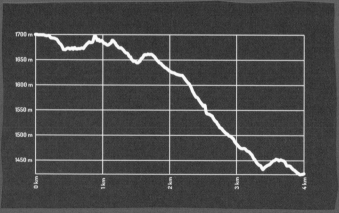

Muggestutz: Zwergenweg Mägisalp–Bidmi

Mägisalp
(lift station)

Bidmi
(lift station)

3 h

4 km

The trail is only open from the end of June through mid-October

To determine official trail openings, hours of operation, and gondola schedules, please visit the official Haslital Berner Oberland website: www.meiringen-hasliberg.ch

Overview

The two Muggestutz dwarf-themed trails (hikes 7 and 8) are gorgeously constructed paths that adults and children will both enjoy and remember for years to come. The trails encourage children to explore and experience nature in beautiful settings while visiting dwarf houses and observing the lives of the dwarves up close and personal. Each point of interest along the route is posted in three languages.

The trail from Mägisalp to Bidmi is easy to follow with multiple activity stations and, approximately halfway, has a generous picnic area with a walnut-run (like a ball-run – but with a walnut!). Just past the picnic area is a toilet. The perfectly appointed dwarf houses, which children are welcome to explore, bring this trail to life. The detailed hand-sewn dwarf clothes and the maps, all demonstrate a love for this area and this incredible trail.

Though you could attempt to complete both trails (hikes 7 and 8) in a single day, the best way to experience these trails is by taking your time. With impressive alpine scenery, book one or two nights in a local hotel (Hasliberg) and ease into your weekend.

Directions

Exit the Mägisalp lift station, you will see a "Muggestutz" sign and map on your left next to a playground. The trail begins here, leading along the lift station and down the mountain. You will pass a cluster of old farmhouses and then veer left away from the lift and towards the first activity station. The trail becomes steep and zigzags through the forest before arriving at a pasture with a farmhouse below that sells drinks and cheese. The trail continues to descend and meander through a forest on a mix of trail and roads. The gondolas will again become visible with the last portion of the trail leading you along a road to the Bidmi lift station.

Tip

Bergrestaurant Mägisalp offers picnic lunches and grilling items for purchase prior to starting your hike.

Special Features

+ This dwarf-themed trail engages the entire family.
+ A detailed labyrinth for children to explore and a cave for discovering cristals are both available on this trail.
+ Beautiful location with ample photo opportunities.

Be Aware

✦ Pick up the small Muggestutz booklet at any of the lift stations or at your hotel. The small booklet offers an array of helpful information, including maps of each of the two trails.

✦ This is not a stroller-friendly hike. Rather, bring a soft-sided carrier with you for when your little one grows weary.

✦ Remember this is a seasonal trail only. Check the website to determine if the trail is open or closed for the season.

✦ The lift from Bidmi stops running at a designated time, check the timetable before you leave.

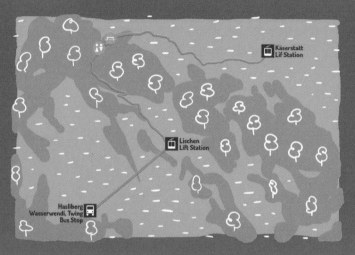

Käserstatt
Lif Station

Lischen
Lift Station

Hasliberg
Wasserwendi, Twing
Bus Stop

picnic/grill spot   toilets

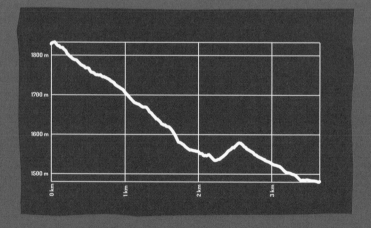

Muggestutz: Zwergenweg Käserstatt–Lischen

Käserstatt
(lift station)

Lischen
(lift station)

---

2 h

3.6 km

The trail is only open from the end of June through mid-October

To determine official trail openings, hours of operation, and gondola schedules, please visit the official Haslital Berner Oberland website: www.meiringen-hasliberg.ch

Overview

This special theme trail meanders through forests and scenic moors. The highlight of the Zwergenweg Käserstatt–Lischen trail is the incredible picnic spot. Perched along a small stream equipped with firewood, grill pits, and plenty of activities to keep children of all ages engaged, this area is worthy of a few hours. As you depart, don't forget to snap a photo of your children on the hanging bridge.

Directions

Exit the Käserstatt lift station keeping to your left. The start of the trail is clearly visible with a colorful archway marking its start. The trail gradually descends through an alpine swamp and past farmhouses. Once in the forest, look for signs depicting dwarfs and enjoy the activities along the way. Approximately halfway, there is an extensive grilling area with a toilet by a river. The trail continues, zigzagging through the forest, and depositing you onto a road leading towards the Lischen lift station. Take the lift down to Twing where connections are available at the Hasliberg Wasserwendi, Twing bus stop.

Tip

On this trail there is a small stream that flows through the picnic area. Bring a change of clothes and let children play in the water!

Special Features

+ This dwarf-themed trail and the dwarf homes will engage the entire family.
+ The trail comes to life with the detailed knitted clothes of the dwarves.
+ Allow plenty of time for children to pull themselves across a cable car which offers a thrilling experience.
+ Ample family photo opportunities.

Be Aware

+ Pick up the small Muggestutz booklet at any of the lift stations or at your hotel. The small booklet offers an array of helpful information, including maps of each of the two trails.
+ This is not a stroller-friendly hike. Rather, bring a soft-sided carrier with you for when your little one grows weary.
+ Remember this is a seasonal trail only. Check the website to determine if the trail is open or closed for the season.
+ The lift from Lischen stops running at a designated time, check the timetable before you leave.

📷 viewpoint   👥 toilets

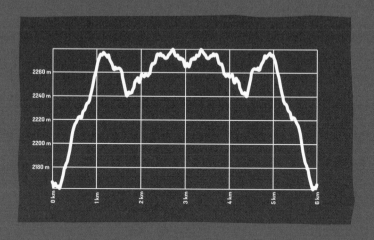

First to Bachalpsee

First (Grindelwald)
(gondola station)

First (Grindelwald)
(gondola station)

3 h
(allow some time to picnic at the lake)

6 km

Summer through fall

Overview

Grindelwald is a charming alpine village, which captivates visitors from the moment one arrives in this small, yet bustling town. With some of the most iconic of the Swiss peaks - Mönch, Eiger, and Jungfrau - visible in the distance, visitors should take the gondola from the village of Grindelwald up to Bort, exit the gondola, and allow their children to play at the incredibly designed Bort playground. Adults may enjoy a coffee or a meal on the Berghaus Bort terrace, while the children frolic and discover. Once the children have grown tired of playing (is that even possible?) get back on the gondola and go up to First (gondola station).

Directions

From the First gondola station, the yellow trail markers will be visible; follow them towards Bachalpsee. The trail offers stunning views throughout its length. The first part of the walk is uphill, but levels out after a switchback. This hike is well-maintained and marked, however, there are a couple of spots that do require extra parental supervision. You can return to the First gondola station by following the markers in the direction you came from.

Trail Markers

First ›› Bachalpsee ›› First

Tip

Pack a picnic and enjoy Bachalpsee as the perfect backdrop. If you are a family that sends out holiday cards, consider Bachalpsee as the perfect backdrop for that special photo.

Special Features

+ Playground, toilet, and restaurant at the Berghaus Bort lift station.
+ Playground, toilet, and restaurant at First.
+ The First Cliff Walk is available for those interested in seeing the mountains from a different perspective. This is a seasonal experience, check for opening times.
+ Amazing views at Bachalpsee.
+ First Flyer zip-line (for adults and older children).

Be Aware

+ Though you may see strollers on this hike, the hike is easier to navigate without.
+ There are several sections of this hike that run close to the edge of the mountain. This should not be a deterrent for the walk; however, parents should use caution with children in these locations. We typically harness our children for safety in areas that are unknown.
+ After leaving the First gondola station there are no longer bathrooms available, nor water stations.
+ The gondola stops running at designated times, check the timetable before you leave.
+ Never attempt this hike in poor weather conditions.
+ Be aware that snow may still be present on this route during the early summer weeks.

Spiez
Train Station

WWII
Bunker

Faulensee
Train Station

 playground castle toilets

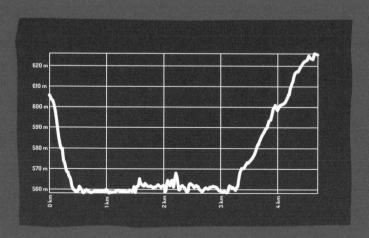

Spiez Lake Walk

Faulensee
(train station)

Spiez
(train station)

1.5–2 h

4.7 km

Year round
However, it is best enjoyed in the spring through fall.

Overview

This marvelous, flat, leisurely walking path seems to have it all. Lake Thun, with its crystal-clear waters, spreads out before you and, on a hot day, you can easily stop along the trail and enjoy a refreshing swim, so pack your bathing suits, a towel, and plenty of sunscreen. The views of the Bernese Oberland stretch out in the distance and both adults and children will enjoy this scenic area.

Children will be engaged from the time the hike starts in Faulensee, as there is a lively playground perched right on the shore of the lake.

The walk concludes in the pristine town of Spiez, with its terraced vineyards setting the stage for a gorgeous photo. Once in Spiez there is another big playground and toilet facilities, allowing families the joy of spreading out a picnic blanket and marveling at the views.

If you still long for more walking, plan to walk up to the Spiez Castle, which offers commanding views of Lake Thun, perfectly maintained gardens, and a small café.

Directions

This walk starts in Faulensee. Exit the train and follow the yellow trail marker sign for "Strandweg," the first set of yellow trail markers is in front of the train station. The trail begins just off the road to the left of a house, and continues straight down through a field towards the lake. After the field, the trail doglegs left and then right and meanders to the lake. Once at the lake, the trail continues along the lake edge until the town of Spiez where you will see a beach area, sand volleyball courts, a park, and play area. From there, follow the markers towards "Schloss" or towards "Spiez, Bahnhof."

Trail Markers

Faulensee ≫ Strandweg ≫ Spiez ≫ Spiez Bahnhof

Tip

In Faulensee, there is an old World War II bunker disguised as a farmhouse – can you find it? Look to your left as you descend towards the lake. You can take a tour on the first Saturday of each summer month. For more information visit: *www.artilleriewerk-faulensee.ch*

Special Features

+ Toilets are available at the start (Faulensee, at the lake) and end of the walk (Spiez).
+ Two playgrounds, one at the start of the walk in Faulensee and one at the conclusion of the walk in Spiez.
+ Scenic and easy for hikers.

Be Aware

+ If driving, park in Spiez and take the train to Faulensee. Not all trains stop at Faulensee, so check the train schedule in advance.
+ This is a stroller-friendly hike. The path is low and paved. Be aware, however, that at the start of the walk, when exiting the train in Faulensee, there are a few steps to navigate.
+ Pack a sufficient amount of water for this walk.

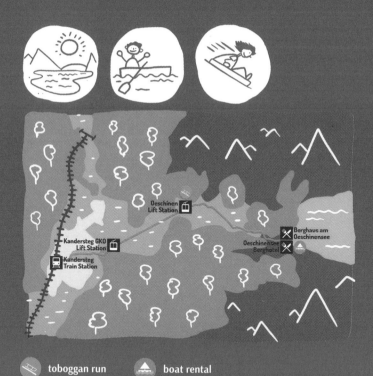

toboggan run   boat rental

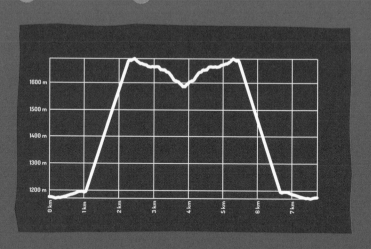

Kandersteg to Oeschinensee

Kandersteg
(or take Bus 242 to Kandersteg, Talstation Oeschinen)

Kandersteg
(or from Kandersteg, Talstation Oeschinen, Bus 242)

2 h
(allow some time to play at the lake)

5.3 km

Virtually year round, though the lake may freeze in winter
Always check the gondola schedule prior to starting your journey.

Overview

The town of Kandersteg, though relatively small, has a cozy alpine feel, but the true essence of this area is high above the village at Oeschinensee. This hike takes you out of the town and up to the incredible Oeschinensee, where views are vast, the lake is calm, and individuals can engage in a multitude of activities.

Directions

From the Kandersteg train station, follow signs to the Kandersteg-Oeschinen Talstation (Gondelbahn) for approximately 1.2 km. Take the lift to the top. The gondola ride up to Oeschinen takes roughly 8 minutes. Once off the gondola, the signs will direct you along an easy-to-follow path to Oeschinensee for another 1.6 km. This path, in winter, is a groomed hiking and snowshoe trail. You can return to Kandersteg train station by following the markers in the direction you came from.

Tip

Stay the night at Berghotel Oeschinensee (open mid-May through October) and absorb the fresh air and gorgeous views. Consider renting a boat and enjoy being on the lake. In winter months bring a sled for additional fun.

Special Features

+ The lake is gorgeous and offers a refreshing place to splash and swim during the heat of summer.
+ Boats are available for rent for those who want to experience the lake first-hand and numerous hiking options are available from the lake.
+ The area offers an exhilarating summer toboggan run (closed November–May due to snow).
+ There are two mountain huts with beautiful views of the lake that offer meals, toilets, water, and lodging. Check opening times and availability of huts prior to starting your journey.
+ Sledding is possible in the area during winter months.

Be Aware

+ The hike is stroller-friendly, however, be prepared to put the stroller on the gondola.
+ Water is not available during this hike; pack plenty.
+ In winter, be aware of skiers and the hiking/snowshoe/ski trails that cross walking paths and hiking trails.

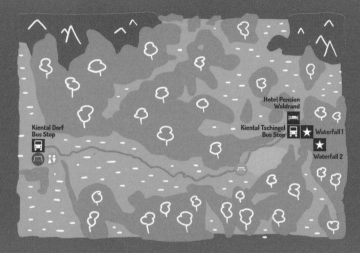

Hotel Pension
Waldrand

Kiental Dorf
Bus Stop

Kiental Tschingel
Bus Stop

★ Waterfall 1

★
Waterfall 2

🚇 playground   🔲 picnic/grill spot   👥 toilets

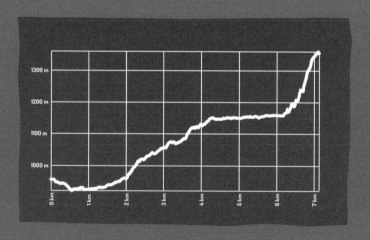

Kiental Dorf to Pochtenalp Berghaus Waldrand

Kiental, Dorf
(bus stop)

Hotel and Pension Waldrand–Pochtenalp
(this is not a public transportation stop)

4 h

7.2 km

Summer through fall
The Berghaus is only open seasonally; check the website prior to starting out on your hike: www.nostalgiehotel.ch

Overview

Kiental is a small valley with impressive views. With only about 210 residents, the village of the same name is located at the end of the valley and this area is peaceful and relaxing. This is not a popular destination, so individuals will enjoy the remoteness and tranquility of the area. Though the walk to Hotel and Pension Waldrand-Pochtenalp is long, there are several opportunities to stop, enjoy a picnic, or cool off in one of the small streams. The last stint of the hike leads walkers past the impressive Gries Gorge and Pochtenfall. Watch your step as the trail is often wet due to the mist from the falls and therefore, may be a bit slippery.

Directions

From the Reichenbach im Kandertal train station, take the number 220 bus to Kiental Dorf. You can also take the bus to the stop Kiental, Ramslauenen and begin the hike from there, which will shorten the hike, but only slightly. Follow trail markers towards Faulbrunni/Pochtenalp, past the flat wetlands and begin your walk through forests, up a couple of hills, past small streams, and finally make your way to the waterfall (Pochtenfall) and up to Hotel and Pension Waldrand-Pochtenalp. The last 2 km are quite steep, so plan accordingly. To return, hike using these directions in reverse or shorten the hike by using any of the bus stops along the way (schedule permitting).

Trail Markers

Kiental ≫ Faulbrunni ≫ Pochtenalp

Tip

Stay the night at Hotel and Pension Waldrand-Pochtenalp. Reserve your accommodation in advance, as space is limited.

Special Features

+ Enjoy the beauty of Pochtenfalls.
+ For those not inclined to hike the entire duration of the walk, bus stops are indicated along the trail, however, the bus is only available during certain times of the year. Check the schedule if you intend to rely on the bus.

Be Aware

+ This is not a stroller-friendly hike.
+ The last portion of this hike is steep, take your time and use caution when climbing.

+ Harnesses may be used on children to provide additional safety near the gorge and waterfall area.
+ Bring plenty of water as we did not come across a place to fill up.
+ This is a long hike so an overnight stay is advised. If the intent is to hike to Hotel and Pension Waldrand-Pochtenalp, make reservations in advance and make sure the mountain house is open for guests, as the hotel is seasonal only.

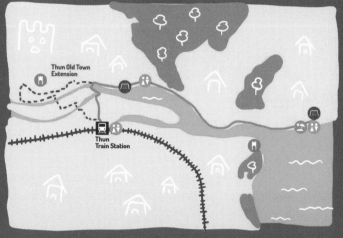

Thun Old Town
Extension

Thun
Train Station

 playground   beach   castle

toilets

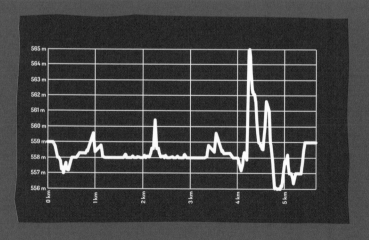

Thun Lake Walk

 13

Thun, Bahnhof
(train station)

Thun, Bahnhof
(train station)

2.5 h

5.7 km

Year round

Overview

Thun is a destination that most people seem to pass through as they make connections to other locations. But stop in Thun and enjoy the lively downtown, especially on a Saturday when the cafés are teeming with people and the streets are spirited!

For a lovely stroll, from the train station simply follow the yellow trail markers to Hünibach and make your way along the scenic Aare River which ultimately leads to Lake Thun.

With the gorgeous river and the lake that is always in view, two playgrounds to keep your children occupied along the way, plus ample opportunities to jump into the lake for a refreshing swim, this easy, yet enjoyable walk is a real pleasure. The walk is not too strenuous and just long enough for a relaxing day trip. Families are encouraged to pack a picnic and a blanket, spread out along the shores of the lake, and enjoy the mountains in the distance.

The walk is remarkably stroller-friendly but be aware that there is little shade along the route. Be prepared with sun protection and plenty to drink.

Directions

From the train station, simply follow the yellow trail markers towards and across the river via a covered wooden bridge and over a small bridge on the right. Continue right in the direction of Hünibach (upstream) and make your way along the scenic Aare River which ultimately leads to Lake Thun. The walk takes you along the lake until you arrive at a crop of bushes where the playground sits back in a green space to your left. To return to Thun train station return on the path along which you arrived.

Trail Markers

Thun Bahnhof ≫ Hünibach ≫ Thun Bahnhof

Tip

During the summer months, bring bathing suits and towels and enjoy a swim in a safe, designated area located at Hünibach.

Special Features

✛ This is a scenic and flat walk.
✛ There are two great playgrounds along this walk, both with toilets in close proximity. One playground is just as you cross over the wooden bridge in Thun and is perched on a hill overlooking the river. The view from the playground is beautiful

and with plenty of benches sitting under shaded trees; parents can sit quietly and enjoy the serenity of the river and lake while the children play.

+ The second playground is located at the end of the walk at Hünibach. There is a toilet located by the small kiosk.
+ Water is available along the route.
+ Hidden behind some bushes at Hünibach is an entrance to the lake. The water is shallow and allows individuals to walk in safely and enjoy the water.

Be Aware

+ This walk is stroller-friendly.
+ Full sun exposure on sunny days.
+ No grilling options available.

/ᴍ\ playground   🏖 beach   🏰 castle

🍴 picnic   🚻 toilets

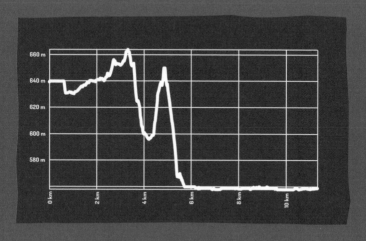

Amsoldingen to Thun

Amsoldingen, Kreuz
(bus stop)

Thun, Bahnhof
(train station)

5 h

11.3 km

Spring through fall

Overview

This impressive hike is a mix of open paths and forests, offering remarkable views of Lake Thun and the Alps on a clear day. This is the perfect hike for a spring, summer, or fall day, with plenty of wild flowers, blooming trees, and lively farms. Once near Lake Thun, children will enjoy Bonstettenpark and plenty of opportunities to swim in the lake. This hike is beautiful throughout and a genuine joy for the entire family. The hike ends at the Thun train station.

Directions

From the Thun train station hop on bus number 3 in the direction of Blumenstein, but get off at the stop Amsoldingen, Kreuz. Once off the bus, cross the street (notice the yellow trail markers on your right), walk along the road in the direction the bus came from and follow the trail markers to Zweiselberg. The first part of the walk takes you through a residential area and then the trail starts with a dirt path. Continue straight and follow the number 4 trail markers indicating Via Jacobi, which is part of the St. James Route within Switzerland. (The hike will continue along the number 4 trail for most of the route.) Be aware that once out of the wooded section, the trail continues along a road for about 5 minutes. Walk carefully and keep the children in close contact. There will be trail markers along the road and then the trail will continue on a protected section that veers to the left down a hill, through a field, and through an underpass. There is a short, steep uphill, which levels out and passes a farm on the left. After the farm, at the trail marker Gwattegg, you can follow the Via Jacobi to the right up to a tree on a hill with picnic benches for a great lunch spot. From here, descend back to the trail marker (Gwattegg) and continue towards Gwatt. This part of the hike parallels the lake which will be on your right, and walks through the Bonstettenpark where the kids will want to play and possibly ask for an ice cream at the kiosk. The path continues to Schloss Schadau (Castle Schadau) and then down the Aare River back to Thun train station.

Trail Markers

Amsoldingen ⟫ Zweiselberg ⟫ Alti Schlyffi ⟫ Gwattegg ⟫ Thun Bahnhof
Part of this hike follows the National #4 trail Via Jacobi (St. James Route)

Tip

Enjoy the Gwattlischenmoos area, which is rich with birds, such as heron and seagulls. Also look for frogs, grass snakes, deer, and the occasional fox. Keep track of the animals you see as you hike.

Special Features

+ Day trip option with alpine views on clear days.
+ Plenty of farms with cows, sheep, and chickens to entertain children.
+ Amazing views of Lake Thun as you near Gwattegg.
+ There is a lovely park (Bonstettenpark) perched right on Lake Thun which offers a climbing structure, swings, sand pit, water station, and a small kiosk with snacks, coffee, and simple meals.
+ A toilet is indicated with white "WC" signs not far from Bonstettenpark.
+ Grilling stations are available just after Bonstettenpark and wood is available onsite.
+ The "Strandbad" (swimming area) in Thun is accessible for a small entry fee.
+ Plenty of opportunities to cool off in the lake.

Be Aware

+ A stroller is possible for this hike but be aware that there are a few uphill sections.
+ Parts of this trail are open and exposed providing little to no shade at all. Plan accordingly by bringing sun hats, sunscreen, and plenty of water.
+ No toilet facilities are available until Bonstettenpark.
+ There are a couple of road crossings and a small section of this hike is on a road with cars and bikes. Use caution when completing this section of the trail.
+ This hike is moderate but may be long for beginners.

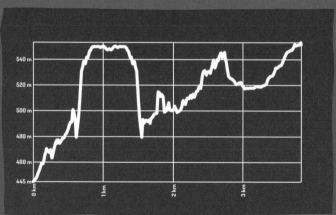

playground	toilets	picnic/grill spot

Taubenloch Gorge

Biel/Bienne, Taubenloch
(bus stop)

Frinvillier–Taubenloch
(train station)

1–2 h

2.9 km
(add 1 km to walk to and from the zoo)

Summer through fall
*The gorge is only open certain times throughout the year; visit the
website for dates when it is open: www.taubenloch.org*

Overview

This hike takes you through the Taubenloch Gorge area, which is perfectly shaded and cool during the hot summer months. Children will be engaged with what this trail has to offer including: the mesmerizing gorge itself, a small zoo, and a playground (slightly off the main trail). The trail is the ideal location for those that long for a new landscape and shade during the height of summer.

Directions

From the Biel/Bienne train station, take bus number 1 or 2 (both buses will take passengers to the necessary stop) and exit at the Taubenloch stop. Cross the street and follow the yellow trail markers for the Taubenloch Gorge. The creek will be on your right. The hike starts at one end of the Taubenloch Gorge and finishes in the town of Frinvillier. Approximately 0.5 km into the hike, the detour to the zoo will be visible by a bridge across the gorge. After visiting the zoo, return to the gorge, continuing upstream to Frinvillier. The final stretch of the walk takes you along a uniquely raised canal and then ultimately up to Frinvillier train station.

Trail Markers

Taubenloch >> Frinvillier

Tip

Take a slight detour off the main trail to enjoy the animals at the small zoo (Tierpark Biel Bözingen) located up the hill.

Special Features

+ A picnic area with a grill is located by the hydroelectric power plant.
+ A playground and grilling space are located outside of the gorge area.
+ There is a small zoo indicated by the trail markers located above the gorge.
+ A playground is available at the end of the zoo – trail markers will indicate this.
+ There is a toilet along the route.

Be Aware

+ A stroller is not recommended on this trail.
+ The trail is often slippery due to the water that moves through the area; hold children's hands and wear sturdy hiking boots. The gorge may be closed during heavy rain.

+ Bring layered clothing as the gorge is often cool, but once outside, the temperature may rise.
+ When the gorge is open, the hours of operation are from 9:00–17:00.
+ Bring food and water for a picnic.
+ There is limited water along the trail.

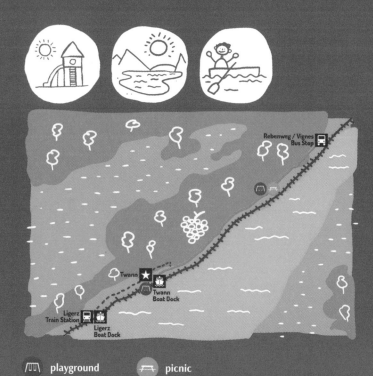

/冊\ playground   ⌒ picnic

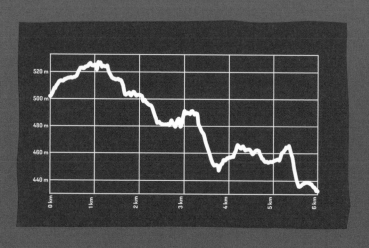

Biel Vineyard Hike

 16

Biel/Bienne, Rebenweg/Vignes
(bus stop)

Twann, Bahnhof
(train station)

3 h

6 km

Spring through fall
Though fall is remarkable when the vineyards are rich with color and the grapes are being harvested.

Overview

This walk is particularly beautiful during the fall months when the vineyards are in full swing and rich with vibrant colors. The views of Lake Biel stretch out before you and on a clear day the Alps are visible. This is a relaxing stroll through vineyards with a small playground available not far from the start of the walk. A picnic area and a grill spot are accessible for those that long to linger and relax before completing this walk.

Directions

From the Biel/Bienne train station, board bus number 11 to the end of the line, Rebenweg/Vignes. Once off the bus you will continue straight through a wooded section, bearing left, and following signs to "Twann 1 h 35 min." You will notice the trail signs indicate, "Rebenweg/chemin du vignoble." Continue on the gravel path until a roadway. At this road, continue left. You will see "Schützenhaus 502 m" on the white section of the trail marker. Follow signs to "Twann 1 h 15 min." There will be a small playground with a picnic and grilling station on your left.

Continue straight on the lower path following trail markers to Twann. You will pass the waypoints of Tüscherz and Roggeten prior to making your way down to Twann on Unterer Chapfweg. You will turn right onto Dorfgasse and continue following the yellow trail markers to the train station which will lead you through the small and charming town of Twann. Make a left onto Hermann J. Fletcher Platz and the train station will be in front of you.

We chose to stay on the lower trail walking the duration of the route through the vineyards. There are other trail markers that indicate alternate routes to Twann, which may be longer and not through the vineyards. For those looking for a longer walk, before dropping down to the town of Twann, follow the yellow trail markers to the town of Ligerz, which is a total of 8.4 km.

Trail Markers

Hüsli ≫ Schützenhaus ≫ Tüscherz ≫ Roggeten ≫ Twann

Tip

A side trip by boat to St. Peter's Island is highly recommended. The Klosterhotel St. Peter has a romantic flare and offers a restaurant with delicious food in a natural setting. There are plenty of opportunities to cool off in Lake Biel.

Special Features

+ There is a small playground with a picnic area and grilling station not far into the hike.
+ This walk offers lovely views of Lake Biel and St. Peter's Island.
+ On a hot sunny day, children will enjoy the numerous lizards on the trail.
+ There is water along the trail.
+ This walk offers incredible opportunities for photographers.
+ There is a playground at the Twann boat station located behind the train station.

Be Aware

+ This is a stroller-friendly walk.
+ The bus from the Biel train station may be located across the street. Look at the map posted on the information board just outside of the train station to determine the bus location.
+ The trail offers little to no shade in warm weather, be prepared with hats, sunglasses, and sunscreen.
+ On occasion, cars will drive along the route; use caution when walking with children.
+ No toilet facilities are available on the walk.

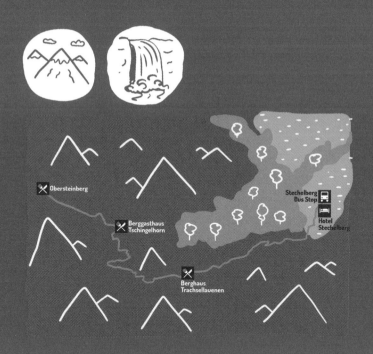

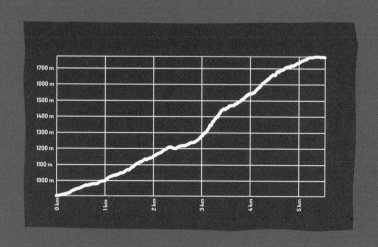

Obersteinberg

Stechelberg, Hotel
(bus stop)

Berghotel Obersteinberg
(this is not a public transportation stop)

3.5 h

5.5 km

June through September
*Berghotel Obersteinberg is seasonal only; contact the hotel to confirm
your reservation and ensure the hotel is open: +41 (0)33 855 20 33*

Overview

Obersteinberg is an untouched area that will leave a lasting impression on its guests. The area is rich with waterfalls and glaciers and encourages you to step back in time and relish in the natural world. This special location is only accessible by foot and helicopter, making it a true escape.

Reserve a room in advance at the Berghotel Obersteinberg and enjoy a relaxing evening and the lack of modern-day conveniences which adds to the charm of your experience. The hike is challenging and mostly uphill from Hotel Stechelberg but the views and the tranquility will reward hikers upon their arrival. There are two additional mountain houses (Berggasthaus Trachsellauenen and Berggasthaus Tschingelhorn) along the route, which, when open, offer meals, water, toilet facilities, and lodging.

Directions

From the bus stop Stechelberg, Hotel, follow the yellow trail markers to the left, up the river. The trail will continue and cross the river within the first kilometer and join a road with a small switchback. Stay on the road until it straightens and continue towards Trachsellauenen (Berghaus). After the Berghaus Trachsellauenen, the yellow trail becomes a White-Red-White mountain trail and forks after 0.5 km. We recommend taking the right trail towards Berghaus Tschingelhorn. This section, approximately 1.4 km in length, begins with gradual switchbacks which become shorter and more frequent until you see Berghaus Tschingelhorn. From here, the trail levels, straightens out, and emerges above the tree line with Obersteinberg approximately 1 km away.

Follow these directions in reverse to make the return journey. This will double the distance of the hike for a total of 11 km. Note that we hiked this route with our children in one day – up and back. We do not recommend Obersteinberg as a day trip, rather, take your time hiking up and relaxing for the night at the hotel. Trust us, everyone will be much happier!

Trail Markers

Hotel Stechelberg >> Trachsellauenen >> Obersteinberg

Tip

The Berghotel Obersteinberg runs their own small dairy farm and with luck (simply stop in the hut on your right as you approach the hotel), you might have the opportunity to witness the cows being milked and cheese being made. Children will adore this educational alpine experience.

Special Features

+ This area is serene and devoid of crowds. It is part of the UNESCO Swiss Alps Jungfrau-Aletsch World Heritage Site.
+ Berghotel Obersteinberg is a special location that encourages a natural slowing down and begs individuals to become one with nature.
+ Look for Steinbock (Alpine ibex) in the area.
+ For another glorious hike and beautiful views, consider making your way up to Oberhornsee from Obersteinberg.

Be Aware

+ This is a White-Red-White trail.
+ This hike is recommended for experienced hikers only and though only 5.5 km in length, the trail is challenging and mostly uphill.
+ The hike up is very steep; consider hiking with poles and keep children in close proximity at all times or use harnesses on this route for additional safety.
+ This hike is not stroller-friendly. Bring a carrier for smaller children.
+ There are steep drop-offs in some areas.
+ There is only one water trough along the route; pack plenty of water for the entire duration of the hike.
+ There are no toilets on this route except for the mountain houses along the way, which also serve meals.
+ The Berghotel Obersteinberg does not have electricity or running water for showers. Dress warm, and pack layers for overnight stays.

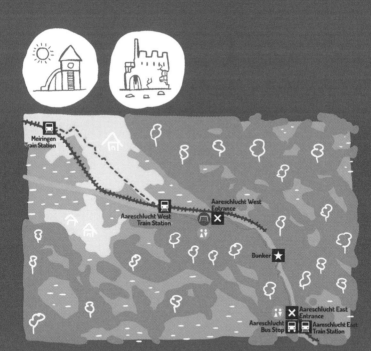

/◫\ playground   👥 toilets

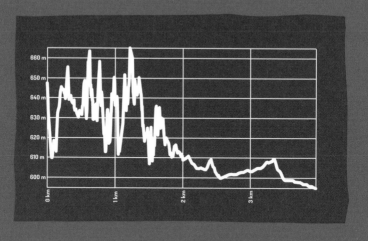

Aare River Gorge Walk

Aareschlucht, Ost
(bus stop)

or

Aareschlucht Ost MIB
(train station)

Aareschlucht West
(train station)

---

2 h

2.3 km
(+1.5 km to Meiringen Bahnhof)

April through November
The gorge is only open certain times throughout the year;
visit the website for dates when it is open: www.aareschlucht.ch

Overview

The Aare River Gorge is a unique location that captivates as it cools and has been a tourist attraction since 1888. The rushing water of the Aare river has traveled from high in the Grimsel area of Switzerland, having melted from the Unteraar Glacier, passing dams and hydroelectric plants, and continues its journey through this chasm, having cut away rock up to 180 m deep in some areas. Did you know it takes 11 minutes for the water to travel 1.4 km through the gorge? The trail, mostly built into the rock face of the gorge, gently winds with the river, becoming narrower and going through some tunnels. Just before the end, the walls are so close you can touch both sides of the gorge. As if the river has not shaped the rocks enough, so have the Swiss by constructing the Meiringen/Innertkirchen railroad tunnel (including a train stop within the tunnel). For those with a keen eye, there is a secret World War II bunker, accessible (at the time) by boating down the gorge itself or via the train tunnel. This is an interesting and fun walk for the whole family, particularly on hot summer days, when the cooling waters of the Aare create mist and a pleasant climate.

Directions

The start of the walk begins at the east entrance to the gorge, easily accessible via the Aareschlucht, Ost bus stop. Alternatively, for those interested and not minding an uphill walk to the entrance, we suggest arriving at the Aareschlucht Ost MIB train stop, which exits within the tunnel, and crosses a metallic suspension bridge before ascending up to the entrance. There is only one path through the gorge; after approximately 2 km, you will approach the exit and be deposited into the Aareschlucht gift shop and restaurant. From there, continue down-river where you will find a foot bridge crossing over the river, turning right towards the Aareschlucht West train stop. Alternatively, you can turn left after the footbridge and follow the yellow trail markers into Meiringen and towards the Meiringen Bahnhof, approximately 1.5 km from the Aareschlucht West train stop.

Tip

For a different view of the gorge, after 18:00 on some evenings during the week, the gorge is bright with special illumination. More details can be found on the website: *www.aareschlucht.ch*

Special Features

+ Toilets are located at the east and west entrances of the gorge and at the Meiringen Bahnhof.
+ There is a playground located at the west entrance.
+ Food is available for purchase at the west entrance.

Be Aware

+ There is an entry fee to access the gorge.
+ This is a wet environment; no running, and wear clothing that can get wet.
+ The gorge may be closed during peak rain periods or bad weather. Check for opening times and closures prior to your visit.
+ Use caution, respect the path, and do not lean over the railings.
+ Keep children in close proximity during this walk.

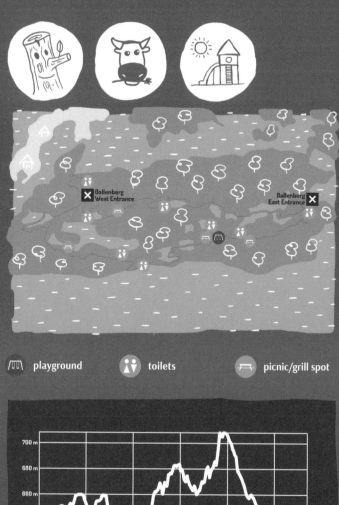

	playground		toilets		picnic/grill spot

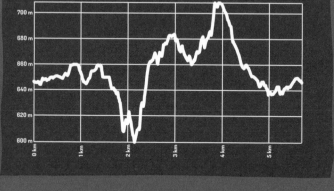

Ballenberg
Open-Air Museum

Ballenberg West, Museum
(bus stop)

or

Ballenberg Ost, Museum
(bus stop)

The museum can be entered from either entrance via the 151 bus.

---

1 day

April through October
The museum is only open certain times throughout the year;
visit the website for dates when it is open: www.ballenberg.ch

Overview

The Ballenberg Open-Air Museum is an outdoor museum that is dedicated to preserving the rich history of the farming and agricultural communities in Switzerland. The museum contains over 100 farm buildings and country homes, all of which are perfectly placed within immaculate grounds.

Though Ballenberg is not a hike, it is far too extraordinary and culturally rich to miss. This open-air museum is a perfect alternative to a traditional hike (though there is a thematic trail all about trees and bushes within the museum grounds) and offers a bit of a refuge in poor weather. With homes and restaurants to slip into during cold or rainy days, families will still have a day in nature, while learning all about Swiss history.

With the "Hands-on House" where children are encouraged to try and touch everything, to games, the petting enclosure, picnic areas, playgrounds, and the enchanted forest, families will be entertained for hours.

Tip

The Ballenberg Open-Air Museum accepts the Swiss Museum Pass. To find out more about the Museum Pass, which provides access to over 300 museums in three countries (Switzerland, Germany, and France), visit the website at: *www.museumspass.com*

Special Features

+ This is the perfect location when the weather is less than favorable for hiking in the mountains.
+ "Nico" is the little boy with the red sweatshirt that points children in the direction of fun. Whenever Nico appears on the map or in front of a particular location, he indicates the area is specifically designed for children.
+ There are over 200 resident animals in Ballenberg.
+ Hands-on activities are available for children of all ages. Visit the website to determine the daily scheduled activities. Some of the activities may include: baking, bread making, weaving, sawing, games, drawing, etc.
+ There are several toilets and restaurants onsite.
+ A theme is selected each year, making the museum all the more captivating for young visitors.
+ Designated picnic areas are available.

Be Aware

+ The grounds are quite expansive and thus, it is not feasible to see all that the museum offers in a single day. Be strategic with your visit and know that you won't see everything.

+ The open-air museum is stroller-friendly, however, the houses, which are on the tour, are not.
+ An ATM is not available onsite. Plan ahead.
+ Lockers for storing luggage are available at both the west and east entrances.
+ Dogs are welcome in the museum; however, they must be kept on a leash.
+ Refer to the website for opening times, as this is a seasonal location: *www.ballenberg.ch*
+ This is the only destination in the book that we arrived at by car.

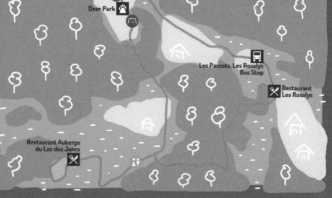

Les Paccots, Ermitage
Bus Stop

Deer Park

Les Paccots, Les Rosalys
Bus Stop

Restaurant
Les Rosalys

Restaurant Auberge
du Lac des Joncs

 playground   toilets

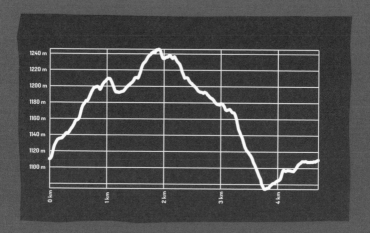

Lac des Joncs Loop

 20

Les Paccots/Les Rosalys
(bus stop)

▷···

Les Paccots/Les Rosalys
(bus stop)

···✕

3 h
(+ play time)

4.7 km

Year round

Overview

This peaceful, wooded hike slowly leads you past a ski area, up to a picturesque lake, and down through a residential area to a lively park for children of all ages to enjoy. The lake, with plenty of benches for picnics, is best enjoyed in the summer months when the sun is high and the pink water lilies are in bloom. Though the lake is not suitable for swimming (it is very deep and swimming is not permitted), enjoy a delightful stroll around the area and consider deviating just off the path to enjoy the large mushroom sculptures just above the back of the lake. To extend the fun, visit the Les Paccots playground located toward the end of the hike. With 10 wooden sculptures (animals, insects, and more), plus interactive information boards, it will help educate children on plants and animals. This play area is a genuine joy for the entire family.

Directions

From the Les Paccots/Les Rosalys bus stop, veer right and up the hill; Hotel Restaurant Les Rosalys will be at the top approximately 200 m from the bus stop. The trail markers will be located ahead on the left (with your back to the hotel) and next to a fence. Follow signs to Lac des Joncs. Go straight through the woods and follow the path past a small chalet, which will be on the left. Continue to follow the yellow trail markers on the trees along the small stream located below the trail on the right. The trail levels and crosses the stream then continues straight until you reach a parking lot for the La Borbuintse Ski Lift and turn left up the road (Route des Joncs). After approximately 200 m, the road will split. Keep right along the road and follow the sign that says, "Auberge du Lac des Joncs." Follow the path up; the lake will be behind a guesthouse and restaurant called Auberge du Lac des Joncs. Enjoy a stroll around the lake, a picnic, or something to eat at Auberge du Lac des Joncs. Descend along the road you came up on, continuing past the La Borbuintse Ski Lift along the road (Route des Joncs). Continue straight through the neighborhood until a wooden climbing structure is visible on the right and a wood-chip path begins. This is the rear of the playground but the adventure can easily start here. Weave your way through the animal sculptures and play areas until the bottom of the playground is reached. After playtime, walk along the sidewalk (heading to your right while looking at the main road, Route des Dailles, from the bottom of the playground) for approximately 750 m until the Les Paccots/Les Rosalys bus stop or turn right up Route des Rosalys to Hotel Restaurant Les Rosalys if staying there.

Trail Markers

Les Rosalys ≫ Lac des Joncs ≫ Les Paccots

Tip

Consider staying at one of the local hotels for easy access to hiking trails. Additionally, consider visiting during the winter months and try snowshoeing on one of the many designated snowshoe paths. The pink trail markers indicate the winter hiking trails and snowshoe paths.

Special Features

+ Toilets are available at Hotel Restaurant Les Rosalys, the Borbuintse Ski Lift, the Restaurant du Lac des Joncs Chalet, and at the bottom (street side) of the playground.
+ Hotel Restaurant Les Rosalys offers a small playground – just big enough to provide quiet time for parents.
+ Food and drinks are available at Hotel Restaurant Les Rosalys and Restaurant du Lac des Joncs Chalet.
+ There is a deer park located by the playground.
+ The playground offers 10 interactive sculpture stations plus multiple play areas.
+ Water is available at the bottom of the park.

Be Aware

+ This is not a stroller-friendly hike.
+ There are exposed roots on the wooded section of the trail.
+ The lake is picturesque, but swimming is not permitted.
+ A good portion of the trail is shaded by trees, making it cool during the hot summer months, but once out of the forest, the road is not shaded.

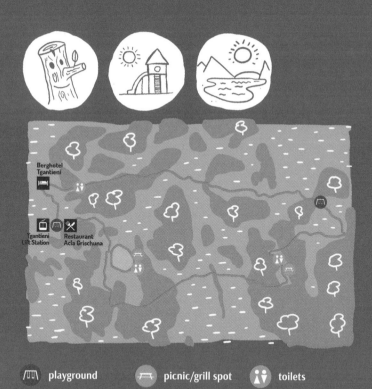

playground · **picnic/grill spot** · **toilets**

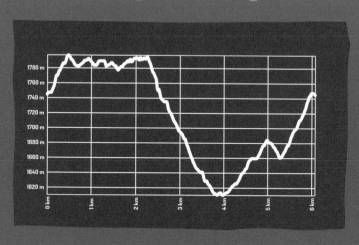

Globi Trail

Tgantieni
(lift station) ▷···

Tgantieni
(lift station) ···✕

2.5 h 🕐

6.1 km 🏃

June through October 📅31

Overview

The Globi Trail, named after the famous Swiss cartoon blue parrot, is a meticulously maintained theme trail, which is a delight for the entire family. This trail may immediately become a favorite for families of all ages. The trail includes 13 interactive stations that educate families on flora and fauna native to the area, and the importance of solar energy, among other hands-on activities. This trail has multiple toilets and grilling areas, which make it the perfect family outing.

Directions

Exit the Tgantieni lift station, turn right heading towards the connecting lift. Turn left up the hill continuing past the lift towards Berghotel Tgantieni. The start of the path will be to your right just below Berghotel. From there, simply follow the white trail markers with Globi indicating the way. There is a moderate hill to the second station. This is the highest point on the trail, which undulates slightly until station seven. The trail descends and turns right after station eight, then continues to descend to station eleven, then it climbs again towards a small winter water reservoir and past two more stations before returning to Tgantieni lift station. The trail is a large loop and will end at the start. To receive a detailed Globi Trail map, either inquire at the Lenzerheide Tourist Information Center or at the bottom of the Tgantieni lift station (Val Sporz).

Trail Markers

Globi Trail or "Globi Wanderweg"

Tip

Right after station seven, there is a fun and interactive play area that informs you about the Rega helicopters that service the Alps for those in need. The bench just below this provides a great view and a box full of books and magazines to enjoy.

Special Features

+ This is an interactive theme trail.
+ There is a playground and restaurant right before station one of the Globi Trail.
+ There are two drinking fountains along the route, located at station six and again at station eight.
+ Toilets are available along the trail at four different stations.
+ Bring lunch for grilling and make use of the several grilling stations along the route.
+ Food is available at Acla Grischuna (a restaurant at Tgantieni lift station) and up the hill at Berghotel Tgantieni.

Be Aware

+ This trail is a White-Red-White trail.
+ This is a stroller-friendly trail.
+ The last chair lift down for the day is at 16:45 during the summer months. Plan your trip accordingly and check the schedule for any changes throughout the year.
+ Station 13 is a slight deviation off the main Globi Trail.
+ The lake at station 12 is not for swimming.

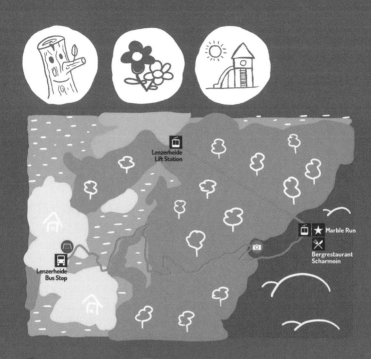

playground   **viewpoint**

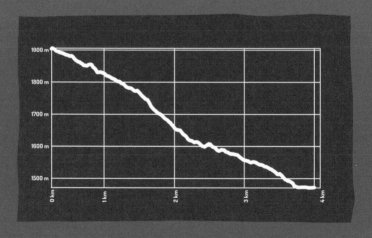

Autschliweg Theme Trail

 22

Lenzerheide/Lai Canols *(lift station)*	
Lenzerheide/Lai, Post *(bus stop)*	
2 h	
3.8 km	
June through October	

Overview

The Autschliweg theme trail, which encourages children to spot the magical bear Autschli, is an engaging trail on well-maintained paths that will keep children walking for the entire duration of the journey. Families are encouraged to discover as many bears as they can along the route. The trail is composed of several stations, they include: a photo point, a place to grill lunch, the perfect spot to relax in the forest on a wooden swing, and a xylophone.

Directions

Take the Rothornbahn gondola from Lenzerheide/Lai Canols lift station to the Middle Station Scharmoin. Exit the Middle Station Scharmoin and turn right towards Bergrestaurant Scharmoin (the trail markers will be clearly visible) to get a starting stamp (you must stamp your Autschliweg card at the start and the finish to receive a small prize). Be cautious of downhill mountain bikers starting their decent into the Lenzerheide Freeride Park. The "Autschliweg" theme trail marker will direct you in front of the restaurant, in the same direction as the mountain bikers but continue past the bike freeride drop-in point. The trail will lead you along a section with great views of the mountains, and then into a wooded section that switches back, continuing the descent. The trail emerges from the woods with the photo station visible and the grill station in the distance. The trail will switch back again and continue the descent along a wider trail that will meander through the woods and narrow at the wooden swing station. The narrow trail becomes a bit steeper, continuing through the wood, then veers left before opening to a wider trail which switches back once more. Below the switchback is the xylophone station and then the trail will turn right. The trail continues down until a road, and the "Autschliweg" trail marker will direct you left down the road. Just after a bend in the road is the finish of the trail with the end-of-trail stamp. Return to Lenzerheide by continuing down the road (be cautious of cars) following the yellow trail markers towards Lenzerheide through a mix of houses and fields. The trail will follow a road to the main road (Voa Principala). Turn left on this road and the Post bus stop will be one block away. The Tourist Information center is right across the road – don't forget to return the stamped card for a small surprise!

Trail Markers

Scharmoin Mittelstation ≫ Autschliweg ≫ Lenzerheide Post

Tip

Don't miss the incredible oversized 250 m marble run with wooden balls at the top of the Middle Station Scharmoin. The wooden balls are available for purchase at the Lenzerheide Tourist Information Center, the Rothornbahn lift station, and at the marble run area for CHF 2 each, and make a nice souvenir. Plan to stay at least one hour at this spot before starting out on the Autschliweg.

Special Features

+ Pick up the Autschliweg card at one of the following locations prior to starting the hike: the Lenzerheide Tourist Information Center, the Rothornbahn Lift station, or at Scharmoin Restaurant for each child in the group. Your child must stamp the card at the start of the trip (there is an orange stamp at the start of the hike located at the Middle Station Scharmoin information board) and again at the conclusion of the hike. Once the trail is complete, children can submit their card at one of three locations indicated on the card to receive a small gift.
+ Children might be interested in watching the mountain bikers begin their journey down the mountain. Allow additional time for this.
+ This trail also coincides with a flower-themed trail for a small portion of the first 0.5 km.
+ Food and water are available at the Middle Station Scharmoin.
+ There were several water fountains along the route.

Be Aware

+ This is a White-Red-White trail.
+ This is not a stroller-friendly route.
+ There is a steep descent after the wooden swing; proceed with caution.
+ Be aware of potential bikers on the trail.
+ Toilets are available at the Middle Station Scharmoin and at the Lenzerheide Post bus station, not along the trail.

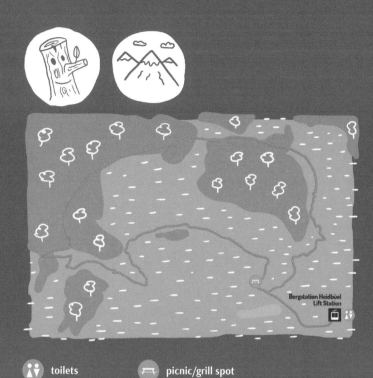

Bergstation Heidbüel
Lift Station

:toilets   picnic/grill spot

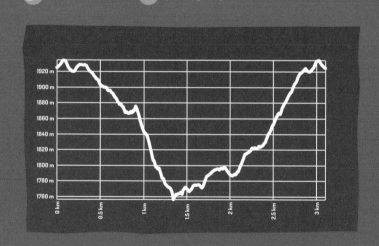

The Weather Path

 23

Bergstation Heidbüel
(lift station)

Bergstation Heidbüel
(lift station)

---

2 h

3.1 km

Late June through mid-October
Check trail opening times before starting your journey.

Overview

The Weather Path in Heidbüel is a ten-station alpine trail created by the wooden weather gnomes. At each station, children must look through a telescope to find and identify a wooden animal in the distance. Once children have identified the animal, they must stamp the correct animal on the "Wetterwichte von Heidbüel" map and stamp card, which is available at the Lenzerheide Tourist Information Center or at the Portal Churwald Lift Station. Children enthusiastically hike from one point to the next to discover the wooden sculptures on the path. Once you complete all ten stations with stamps and solve the mystery phrase, return the card to the Portal Churwald Lift Station to receive a small prize.

Directions

Take the gondola from Portal Churwalden up to Mountain Station Heidbüel. Exit the gondola station to the right and, after the lake, locate the wooden trail markers pointing to the right. The trail is well-marked by wooden trail markers, labeled "Wetterwichtweg." At the start, the trail leads between two large wooden poles, and splits. To the left is the grilling and picnic area and to the right is the start of the trail just after the wooden lounge chairs. The trail begins to descend and is quite steep after stations two and three, which can be precarious in wet weather. Watch where you step! After crossing the stream a second time, the trail begins to climb steadily upwards. Towards the end of the trail, once the lift station becomes visible, turn left to locate the tenth (last) station before continuing up to the lift station.

Trail Markers

Wooden trail markers labeled "Wetterwichtweg"

Tip

This was the only trail where we have ever witnessed multiple black salamanders while hiking. Watch your step and search for these adorable creatures on the path!

Special Features

+ This is a genuine alpine trail with great views.
+ This is a theme trail that is engaging for the entire family.
+ Children must use a telescope to identify wooden animal sculptures throughout the trail. Once they have identified the animal, they must then stamp their maps.
+ There is a grilling station but be aware of any fire bans.
+ Food for grilling is available to purchase during good weather at the Alpbeiz Alp Stätz Kiosk near the start of the hike.

Be Aware

+ This is a White-Red-White trail.
+ This is not a stroller-friendly hike.
+ There are steep ascents and descents during this hike, proceed with caution.
+ There are no bathrooms along the path; use the facilities at the top of Heidbüel before starting the hike.
+ The last lift of the day goes down the mountain at 16:30. Plan accordingly.

Tourist
Information
Lenzerheide
Bus Stop

 playground toilets

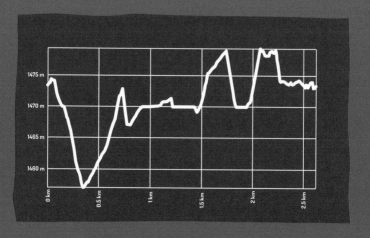

1475 m
1470 m
1465 m
1460 m

0 km 0.5 km 1 km 1.5 km 2 km 2.5 km

Lenzerheide Photo Orienteering Challenge

Lenzerheide Tourist Information Center across from Lenzerheide/Lai, Post
(bus stop)

Lenzerheide Tourist Information Center across from Lenzerheide/Lai, Post
(bus stop)

1–1.5 h

2.6 km

Year round

Overview

The Lenzerheide Photo Orienteering Challenge is a lovely walk through Lenzerheide, and is an ideal way to get to know the town. You will learn interesting facts about the area and Graubünden. Though not necessarily easy, for families that appreciate a good challenge (part scavenger hunt, part quiz) and a trail that is educational, this might just be the perfect way to become better acquainted with this area.

Directions

Obtain the Photo Orienteering Map and information pack from the Lenzerheide Tourist Information Center. You can decide in which direction to start and finish the route outlined on the map.

Trail Markers

This trail is not marked, and does not follow any local signage.

Tip

This challenge is a bit tricky, but fun. For those hard to answer questions, and when a local resident cannot be found, bring your cell phone to look up any answers. Is this cheating? Gosh, we hope not!

Special Features

+ This is a photo orienteering challenge in the town of Lenzerheide.
+ There is a toilet available at the Lenzerheide Post Bus station and again, on the north side of the soccer field on the corner of Voa Sporz and Voa Pintga.
+ Food and water are available at the many restaurants and shops in the town.
+ When you are finished answering all 13 questions from the challenge, turn in your answer sheet to the Lenzerheide Tourist Information Center for your "Lenzerheide Expert Diploma."
+ There are two playgrounds located along the route.

Be Aware

+ This is a stroller-friendly walk.
+ The photo orienteering challenge can be completed in any order, with the map that is available. The photos available with the challenge are there to guide you to the white signposts (20 x 30 cm) with questions in both German and English. The photos contained in the challenge are in no particular order, adding a bit of difficulty to the task.

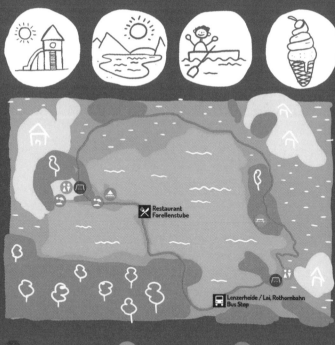

Restaurant
Forellenstube

Lenzerheide / Lai, Rothornbahn
Bus Stop

playground	picnic	beach
boat rental	toilets	

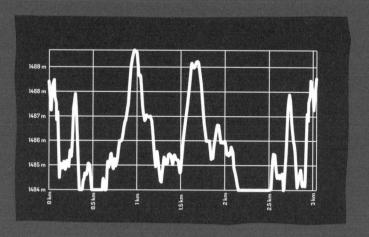

Heidsee Lake Walk

Lenzerheide/Lai, Rothornbahn
(bus stop)

Lenzerheide/Lai, Rothornbahn
(bus stop)

1 h 20 min
(walking time, allow additional time for swimming and playing)

3 km

Summer

Overview

The Lenzerheide region is an incredibly family-friendly destination and warrants a few days to explore the area. The area is rich with outdoor activities and is the perfect summer or winter holiday location. For an easy walk, consider a stroll around Heidsee. This is a delightful path, with its flat trail and the remarkably child-friendly beach area. On a warm day, this is the ideal location to swim, play, and picnic. Children will delight in the opportunity to splash, catch fish, watch ducks, and absorb the true essence of summer.

Directions

From the Rothornbahn bus stop, walk towards the entrance of the Rothornbahn lift station. On your right you will see a road underpass, which will connect you to the lake path. At the lake, make a right and continue along the gray gravel path around the lake. The path is flat and easy to follow. The first playground is approximately 400 m from the underpass and then the trail will continue around the lake to the left of Kiosk Canols and the playground area. The trail meanders through a small wooded picnic area and then continues veering left around the lake. This stretch of path has minimal to no shade and will veer left once again just before the beach area. Kiosk Lido is on a side path to the right. From the beach area, continue along the main gravel path, which veers right at the Forellenstube Restaurant then left at the main road. The path will make its final right turn and you can continue towards the Rothornbahn lift station, which is clearly visible across the edge of the lake. This walk can be completed in either direction.

Trail Markers

White (local) trail markers listed as "Seerundgang"

Tip

Children will want to swim and play at the large beach area (Lido) on the Lenzerheide side of the lake. Bring bathing suits, towels, and sunscreen.

Special Features

+ This is an ideal walk in the summer months with great mountain views.
+ There are two play areas for children to enjoy, one at the start of the walk (Kiosk Canols) and the second at the beach (Kiosk Lido).
+ Water is available at the two Kiosks.
+ Food is available for grilling and eating at Kiosk Lido.
+ Toilets are also available at both Kiosk areas, along with showers.

Be Aware

+ This is a stroller-friendly walk.
+ Part of this walk includes protected nature areas; please respect the animals that are native to the area.

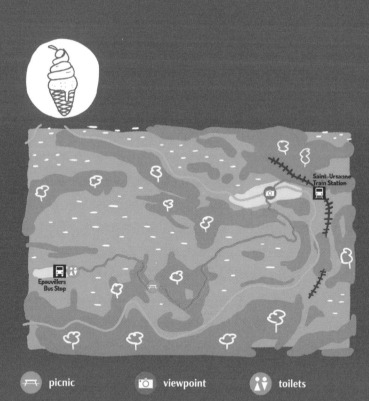

Epauvillers
Bus Stop

Saint-Ursanne
Train Station

🚏 picnic   📷 viewpoint   🚻 toilets

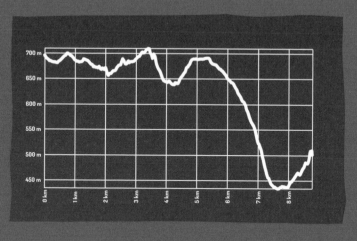

Epauvillers to Saint-Ursanne

Epauvillers, Poste
(bus stop)

Saint-Ursanne
(train station)

3.5 h

8.8 km

Year round

Overview

This trail, located in the Jura Mountains, is full of lush, rolling hills and expansive views. The magic of this hike starts in the early morning hours. Observe the dew-drops all over the grass and hills, as well as the captivating spider webs illuminated by the moisture. Rocky and grass trails fill the walk, which leads you in and out of the forest, and eventually to the Medieval and historic town of Saint-Ursanne. With charming cobblestone streets, the Collegiate Church, and picturesque views of the Doubs River, walkers will feel a sense of accomplishment while enjoying a coffee or ice cream in this delightful little town.

Directions

Take the train to Saint-Ursanne. Exit the train and board bus number 62. Once on the bus, exit at the Epauvillers, Poste bus stop. At the stop to the left there are trail markers indicating the route to Saint-Ursanne. Heading back in the direction the bus came from, the trail will follow the road for approximately 150 m before heading through a field. The trail will continue briefly on a road and then through a forest towards Montenol. This is a small farming town but be aware of cars on this road. The trail will meander downwards before turning left towards Saint-Ursanne. Be aware, there is a road crossing on this section so exercise caution when crossing with children. The trail will open up and reveal the town of Saint-Ursanne. Enjoy the town before heading up to the train station approximately 1 km away.

Trail Markers

Epauvillers ≫ Saint-Ursanne (via Montenol)

Tip

Consider bringing a scavenger hunt for this hike, as it is long and there are no play-grounds along the route (you'll find one in the final chapter of the book).

Special Features

+ Incredibly magical on an early morning in the fall, with picturesque fog, bright colors, and open views.
+ A pleasant opportunity to see the Jura Mountains on a relatively flat trail.
+ The hike ends in the extremely photogenic town of Saint-Ursanne.
+ Food options are available in Saint-Ursanne.
+ Picnic area available midway on the trail and in Saint-Ursanne along the Doubs River.
+ Toilet at the start of the hike, follow the sign to "WC" indicated at the bus stop.

Be Aware

+ This hike is not stroller-friendly.
+ The trail is comprised of rocky and grassy trails.
+ Caution, some of this trail takes you along/across roads; walk with care.
+ Part of the trail has steep drop-offs, however, this should not be a deterrent for the trail, as it is wide and children can easily walk on the inside.
+ The final stretch to the Saint-Ursanne train station can seem long; prepare for the short stretch of road with a slight incline.
+ No water available on the trail.
+ No designated play areas or picnic areas available, however, there were two picnic benches along the walk.

playground   **toilets**

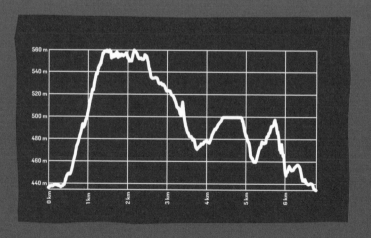

Weggis to Hertenstein

Weggis
(boat dock)

Hertenstein
(boat dock)

2.5 h

6.3 km

Year round

Overview

This scenic hike offers commanding views of Lake Lucerne and the surrounding mountains. Once off the train in Lucerne, board the Weggis/Vitznau boat for a unique and up-close experience on the lake.

This hike has a steady climb at the beginning making it unsuitable for strollers. Part of the trail is exposed so plan accordingly when hiking on hot, sunny days. The views from the majority of this hike are impressive and there are several benches along the route allowing walkers to stop and take in the majestic lake and layered mountains in the distance.

Hike down to Hertenstein, over grassy sections and through densely wooded forests. Once out of the forest, there are open trails, which lead down a few stairs to the small area of Hertenstein where you can catch the return boat back to the Lucerne train station.

Directions

Disembark the boat at Weggis and follow the yellow trail markers towards the Weggis Luftseilbahn. There is a small school at the start of the hike, which offers a modest playground for children interested in playing prior to starting the route. Up from the Luftseilbahn, the trail cuts through a field before turning left on a road (Zingelistrasse) in the direction of Untereggi. From Untereggi, a village of small farm houses, the trail continues right along a road (Untereggistrasse), which merges with Remsistrasse and deposits you at a roundabout. Follow the yellow trail markers through the roundabout, turning right at the next street (Röhrlistrasse) then left onto Hügeristrasse. Follow the yellow trail markers towards Hertenstein, which will lead you through fields, down a small hill, past a farm, through woods, and to the boat dock in Hertenstein. This hike can easily be completed in reverse order.

Trail Markers

Luftseilbahn ≫ Gribsch ≫ Untereggi ≫ Hertenstein

Tip

To make the most of your day, plan to take the steamboat from Lucerne to Weggis. The boat trip is highly entertaining for children and adults alike. This experience will add another source of entertainment for the children. In Hertenstein, stop for an ice cream or a coffee at Café Vienna and enjoy the marvelous views while waiting to board the boat back to Lucerne.

Special Features

+ Incredible views of Lake Lucerne and an opportunity to take a boat on it.
+ A playground at the start of the hike at the local school (Schule Weggis) located on Rigistrasse.

Be Aware

+ This is not a stroller-friendly hike.
+ There is a small portion of this hike that takes hikers through the main road in Weggis, so use caution when crossing roads. This portion of the hike is roughly 5–10 minutes and quickly leads back onto protected trails, away from traffic.
+ No water is available on the hike. Make sure to pack plenty.
+ Check the boat schedule before heading out on your hike and try to plan your departure and return accordingly.

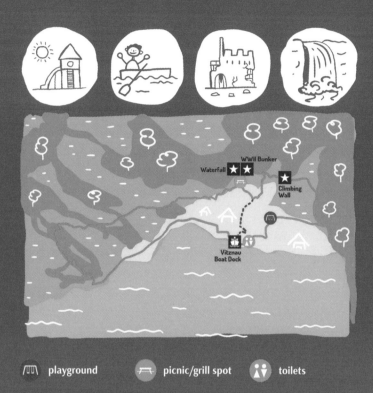

playground   picnic/grill spot   toilets

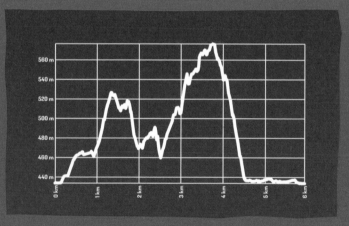

Vitznau Circular Walk "Vitznauer Rundweg" 28

Vitznau
(boat dock)

Vitznau
(boat dock)

3 h

5.9 km
This is a moderate or easy hike (if it is cut short at the waterfall).

Spring through fall

Overview

This pleasant, scenic hike makes for a perfect family day trip. From the Lucerne train station board the boat to Vitznau. Once on the boat, enjoy the views that spread out before you of Lake Lucerne and the surrounding mountains. Children are happy to walk the three hours as they have the opportunity to play at a playground, hike up through a forest, and climb on a climbing wall at the dam. With a slight detour, a waterfall and small pond are accessible. Though the waterfall is not part of the trail, the area will provide children with the opportunity to play and cool off on hot days. The trail ends back in the picturesque town of Vitznau.

Directions

This hike is marked by the white trail blazes indicating "Rundweg Promenade." Once off the boat and facing the Rigi Kulm Cogwheel Railway, head to your right. The first point of interest is the historic hotel Vitznauer-Hof. From here, the trail slowly climbs uphill leading walkers to an enclosed and wonderful playground with a water station for children. After families have enjoyed playing, continue to climb up, past the mobile home camp and up through the forest where you will encounter hanging chairs. As walkers continue, they will come to an area that offers wood and a fire pit for grilling plus a small climbing wall for children to play. After this section, the trail leads walkers along a road so proceed with caution. There is a waterfall (Mülibachfall) at 2.1 km, which provides another area for children to play and cool off. At this point, individuals may opt to turn back and follow the yellow trail markers back to the Vitznau boat dock as the kid-centric aspects of this hike are essentially complete after the waterfall. For those who continue, follow the trail past a farm to arrive at the Rigi Bahn Cogwheel train tracks. Look for the train and cross with caution! Turn right at the road, continuing along it for approximately 1.5 km. Turn left just after a farm house; this path will descend to the main waterfront road (Seestrasse). Be careful crossing this main road! Turn left at this road and continue along it until arriving at the Vitznau boat dock.

Special Features

+ Ideal for children thanks to a playground, tree swings, and a climbing wall.
+ Grilling station with wood and a picnic table.
+ A chance to see the Rigi Kulm Cogwheel Railway.
+ A public toilet is available at the boat dock in Vitznau. It is recommended you use the facilities before starting the walk.
+ Plenty of benches and areas to rest along the way.
+ 11 points of interest along the walk, which are clearly outlined in the map available at the Tourist Information Station right across from the boat dock.

Be Aware

+ This is a local trail; part of this hike is on a White-Red-White trail.
+ This is not a stroller-friendly hike.
+ Sections of this hike are on roads without sidewalks. Please walk with caution.
+ There are no water stations to fill up once on the trail.
+ No toilet facilities once on the trail.
+ Make sure the boat you have boarded stops in Vitznau.
+ For your return by boat or bus, plan your route and time accordingly.

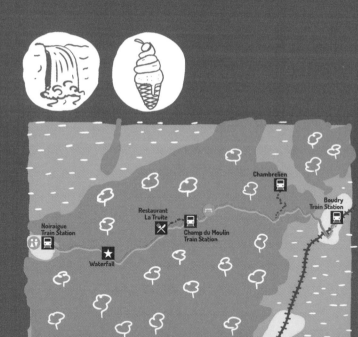

picnic/grill spot toilets

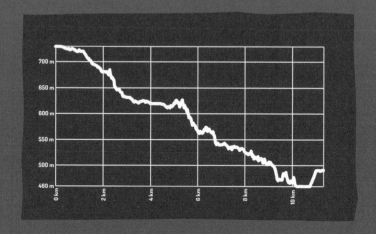

Areuse Gorge

 29

Noiraigue
(train station)

Boudry
(train station)

4–5 h

11.4 km

April through November
The hike is cooling in the summer and scenic in the fall.

Overview

The Areuse Gorge offers a varied landscape not often seen in Switzerland and provides a secluded hike along the river that has carved and sculpted the rock over many centuries. The trail provides benches and picnic areas and is best enjoyed over the course of an entire day. This route offers two cutout points, making the journey shorter if needed but the entire length should not be missed if the child(ren) can handle the distance. This hike is a hidden gem.

Directions

From Noiraigue train station, turn right onto the road (Rue des Tilleuls), which parallels the train tracks. Continue down this road turning right at the end (onto Rue de l'Areuse). Take the small path on the left just before the train tracks. Continue along until the first train track crossing, crossing the rails and then turning left to continue along the train tracks. The gorge trail begins 0.5 km after the railway crossing when the trail drops down to the river and continuing past a hydroelectric station. Cross the bridge over the river and enjoy the descent through the narrow gorge (with a nice photo opportunity) and over the famous Bridge Saut de Brot. The trail, leveling to the river and continuing past a second hydroelectric station, follows a road until it reaches a cluster of buildings including a café. This is Champ du Moulin (Field of the Mill). At the end of this road the trail continues right (yellow trail marker indicating "Autres directions") and over a bridge. See Cutout 1.

Once over the bridge, where you'll find another café and hotel, continue along the river. The trail will cross the river over another bridge into a wooded section with stairs up and then back down to the river. At this spot, the trail begins to cross one of three bridges that all connect, keep left and continue down the river. Soon after, the trail crosses the river again and then turns left off a dirt road and into the forest. This is a nice spot to picnic or grill. The trail continues past this picnic area and places you back on the road from which you deviated. After approximately 0.5 km, the trail will turn left, dropping back down to the river and crossing a bridge. The trail will lead you back across another bridge after another 0.7 km. The trail will then cross the river again at Pont de Vert (Green Bridge); continue down the river towards Pont des Clées/Boudry. See Cutout 2.

This section of the trail continues between high cliffs and a winding river that culminates and climbs up to a bridge that crosses a narrow slot in the rock. This is an interesting area, which resembles a jungle, before arriving at the Pont des Clées (Bridge of Keys). This bridge is approximately 2 km from the Boudry train station. The trail continues uninterrupted, along the river and through a tunnel, and ends at a parking lot next to a hydroelectric station. You will see a train bridge high overhead; this is approximately 1 km from the Boudry train station. Continue along the road but use caution! The trail leads across a bridge that must be shared with cars. Take the first sharp left after the bridge, which leads directly to the Boudry train station.

Cutout 1

At Champ du Moulin (Field of the Mill), the trail can be cut short by turning left to the Champ du Moulin train station (approximately 550 m away); total hike length 4.9 km.

Cutout 2

At Pont de Vert (Green Bridge), you can follow trail markers to Chambrelien, which progresses up and out of the gorge to the Chambrelien train station; total hike length 9.5 km.

Trail Markers

Noiraigue ≫ Saut de Brot ≫ Champ du Moulin ≫ Pont de la Verrière ≫ Pont de Vert ≫ Pont des Clées ≫ Boudry

Tip

There are two cafés along the trail at Champ du Moulin at 4.5 km into the hike. This is a good spot to pause and enjoy a snack, coffee, hot chocolate, or an ice cream on a hot day!

Special Features

+ An intimate hike through a beautiful area.
+ Picnic and grilling.
+ Toilets are available at the Noiraigue and Champs du Moulin cafés.

Be Aware

+ This is not a stroller-friendly hike.
+ The gorge is wet in many areas and can be slippery on roots, rocks, and metal stairs/walkways. Wear good hiking shoes and appropriate clothing and use caution. It is not advised to hike this trail in the rain.
+ Respect the posted signage for safety.
+ Trail closure or detours may be possible. Check with the local tourist office for up-to-date information.

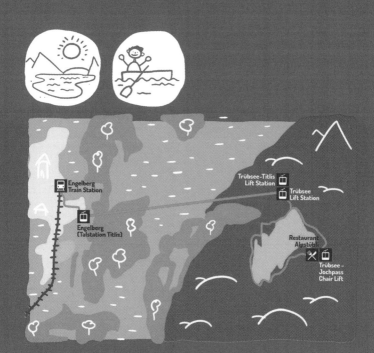

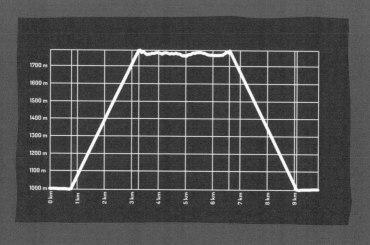

Trübsee Lake Walk

30

Engelberg
(train station)   ▷···

Engelberg
(train station)   ···✕

---

2 h   🕐

4.9 km   🏃

Year round   📅

Overview

This flat, easy hike takes you around picturesque Lake Trübsee. Take your time on this walk as you soak up the views of the mountains. Plan to bring a picnic or food for grilling and enjoy an afternoon in a striking location.

Directions

Exit Engelberg train station to the right. Follow signs towards Engelberg Talstation, turning right down the walkway at the back of a row of houses. Follow this path, which veers left and then deposits you at the main road (Engelbergerstrasse). Cross the road and proceeding down Gerschnistrasse, a large parking lot will be on your left. The Talstation Titlis will be on the right after crossing the river. Take the lift up to the Trübsee lift station. Exit the lift station towards the lake and follow the trail on the right down the hill. The walk can be completed from either direction by following the path around the lake with a return to Trübsee lift station and returning to Engelberg train station.

Tip

For individuals seeking incredible views (on a clear day) and a thrilling walk across the Titlis Cliff Walk, make your way up to Titlis. This area is popular with tourists and year-round skiing is possible. Proceed with caution if taking small children up to Titlis due to elevation, cold temperatures, and sharp drops.

Special Features

+ Beautiful lake and mountain views.
+ This trail is flat so the hiking is easy.
+ Food, toilets, and water available at Trübsee Alpine Lodge prior to starting the hike or at the finish.
+ Grill pits available.
+ Boat rentals available.

Be Aware

+ A stroller is possible on this route, but be prepared to put it on the gondola.
+ The gondola ride from Engelberg is typically crowded with tourists making their way up to Titlis, so be prepared for this. Once off the gondola, the crowds will dissipate.

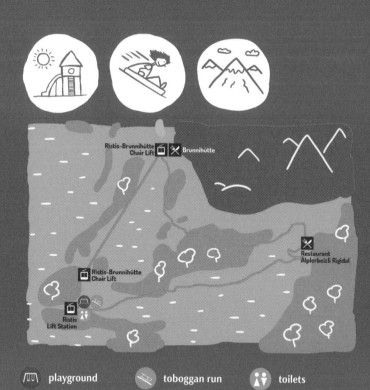

Ristis-Brunnihütte
Chair Lift — Brunnihütte

Restaurant
Älplerbeizli Rigidal

Ristis-Brunnihütte
Chair Lift

Ristis
Lift Station

playground **toboggan run** **toilets**

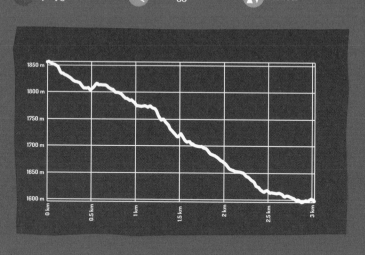

Brunni to Ristis

Engelberg (Brunni-Bahnen)
(lift station)

Engelberg (Brunni-Bahnen)
(lift station)

1 h 20 min

3 km

Year round

Overview

The true wonder of this area is the incredible Globi Children's Playground, named after the famous Swiss cartoon blue parrot, and summer toboggan course at Ristis. This area is a genuine children's paradise and parents will be able to relax and relish the quiet as their children run from one activity to the next. After a long, enjoyable play, make your way via the chair lift, which will sweep you up the mountain to start the hike.

The hike is an easy downhill stroll, offering beautiful mountain views throughout. In the winter months, throw snowballs and bring a sled.

Directions

Take the Brunnibahn to Ristis and continue up the second chairlift to Brunni-hütte. Once off the chairlift you can veer right and begin your walk down towards Rigidalstafel/Ristis. In the summer months you can enjoy a stroll around the small lake (Härzlisee) behind the Brunnihütte. There are several routes down to Ristis; we recommend the yellow blazed trail (45 min) as this is most appropriate for children and offers expansive views of the Engelberg valley. In the winter this is a groomed snow path and along the trail from Rigidalstafel are several wooden benches and swings. Plan to stay awhile at Ristis to enjoy the expansive playground. Continue down to the Engelberg (Brunni-Bahnen) lift station.

Trail Markers

Brünni ≫ Rigidalstafel ≫ Ristis

Tip

For added family enjoyment look for Globi to make an appearance in good weather at the Berglodge Restaurant Ristis during the peak summer season.

Special Features

+ Amazing views throughout the hike.
+ Grilling opportunities are available at the Globi Children's Playground.
+ Food, drink, and toilets are available at both the Berglodge Restaurant Ristis and at the Brunnihütte at the start of the hike.
+ Bring a sled in the winter months and make the most of the downhill trail.

Be Aware

+ This is not a stroller-friendly hike.
+ Water is not available along the route.
+ Always check lift operating times before you start your journey.
+ Toilets are not available along the route.
+ During the winter months, beware of skiers who might cross the path.

playground • **castle** • **toilets**

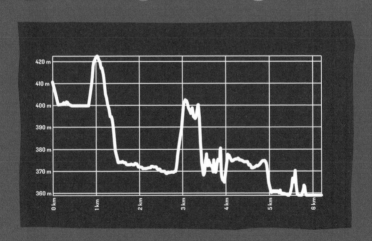

Rhine River Walk

Schaffhausen
(train station)

Schloss Laufen am Rheinfall
(train station)

---

4 h

6.2 km

Year round
The falls are best in July when the water is at its highest.

Overview

This pleasant walk allows you to witness the beauty of the Rhine Falls from a unique perspective. Starting in the picturesque town of Schaffhausen, meander slowly through the pristine streets while taking in the buzz of the town. For those who elect to walk in the summer months and especially on a Saturday, don't bother packing a picnic, rather enjoy the goods at the local market and pick up fresh produce, grilled sausages, and homemade bread from local merchants. After enjoying the old town, walk up to the impressive and well-preserved Munot Fortress dating back to the 16th century. The fortress provides a great opportunity for children to explore and enjoy the walk to the top where cannons await. Views are equally impressive.

Walk back down and experience the rose gardens located just across from the fortress and don't forget to stop at the playground just 250 m from the fortress on Hirschweg.

The walk is rich with activities for children, including three play areas, lovely paths along the Rhine, the impressive Rhine Falls themselves, and Laufen Castle. Prepare to enjoy a day full of activities and marvelous sights.

Directions

Exit the train station in the direction of the old town center (Altstadt) of Schaffhausen. Walk straight through town and make a left onto Vordergasse and then follow signs to Munot Fortress (be prepared to climb lots of steps). Don't forget to stop off at the rose gardens located just across from Munot Fortress. Exit Munot Fortress to the right (not the vineyard side) and walk onto Hirschweg. Walk approximately one block, or 250 m, to locate the playground. To continue, walk back towards Munot Fortress, but veer left onto Römerstieg down the series of stairs and exit to the right once off the staircase. Follow the yellow trail markers to Rheinfall crossing over the bridge. Cross the street and follow the signs for the Via Rhenana 60 trail marker in the direction of Flurlingen and walk along the lower banks of the river downstream. You will pass a spillway/hydroelectric station and then pass under and through a small tunnel. Continue on the trail marker "60" path and up the slight hill, vineyards will be on the left. Turn right onto Gründenstrasse and drop back down to the river. Cross the small bridge once again following trail "60." Follow the footpath called "Fussweg Rheinfall Neuhausen." Follow the trail markers "60" towards Rheinfall Dach. There is a small playground located on the right as well as a small area to dip your feet into the Rhine (use caution with children). Continue on the trail and walk under the bridge to the left, crossing over the big train bridge with the trail parallel to the train tracks. After crossing the bridge, walk up the series of stairs to the left which will take you up to Laufen Castle. At this point, a playground, food options, and toilets are available at the castle. Walk through the castle and down to the left set of stairs descending down toward to the Schloss Laufen train station.

Trail Markers

Schaffhausen >> Schaffhausen Schifflände >> Flurlingen >> Rheinfall

Tip

For added adventure, take a boat to have a closer look at the impressive Rhine Falls. For a different perspective of the falls, cross over the bridges just below or above the falls.

Special Features

+ Toilets are located at: Schaffhausen train station, Munot Fortress (climb to the top), the playground located on Hirschweg, and again at Laufen Castle.
+ Three playgrounds are located along the route, the first down the road from Munot Fortress on Hirschweg, the second along the Rhine, and the third at Laufen Castle.
+ There are plenty of water fountains to fill water bottles.
+ Part of the walk is located right along the banks of the Rhine.
+ Munot Fortress is a gorgeous place to explore. The opening times (admission is free of charge) for Munot Fortress are as follows: May through September 08:00–20:00 and October through April 09:00–17:00.
+ There are boat trips available for purchase at the Rhine Falls from April through October.
+ Food is plentiful and available in the town of Schaffhausen and again near Laufen Castle.
+ For parents looking for a delicious glass of refreshing wine after the walk, try Hallauer, a Riesling-Sylvaner mix from Schaffhausen. A deliciously fresh way to end the day!

Be Aware

+ This is not a stroller-friendly hike.
+ There are lots of stairs to climb should you elect to walk up to Munot Fortress.
+ Part of the walk is extremely close to the Rhine River; you should use caution when walking with children.
+ Parts of this walk take you through small neighborhoods and on roads, so use caution when walking in the road with children.

📷 viewpoint	🏰 castle	🚻 toilets
🛝 playground	🍽 picnic/grill spot	

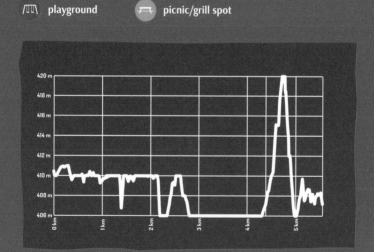

Zurich Lake Walk

Pfäffikon SZ
(train station)

There is another town called Pfäffikon, in the canton of Zurich,
pay attention to arrive at the Pfäffikon SZ (Schwyz) train station!

Rapperswil
(train station)

2 h
(2.5 h with a walk through Rapperswil)

4.4 km
(approximately 5.6 km with a walk through Rapperswil)

Year round
Check the opening hours of the bridge prior to starting out on your
hike: www.zuerich.com

Overview

This pleasant stroll is perfect for families looking for an outing that doesn't require too much effort. With plenty of views of Lake Zurich, a modest playground, plus an expansive wooden foot bridge (the longest wooden bridge in Switzerland), children will enjoy spotting ducks, birds, and fish in the transparent water below. The conclusion of the walk allows you to stroll through the charming town of Rapperswil – a perfect way to end the day.

Directions

Exit the Pfäffikon SZ train station on the lakeside and turn right following the yellow trail markers toward Rapperswil. The trail continues straight along the train tracks and fields. Continue through the Seedamm/Frauenwinkel Nature Preserve. This path will curve left along the nature reserve, and after a small tunnel under the train tracks, there is a playground with picnic and toilet facilities. After the playground, there is a street crossing with traffic lights; watch out for bikes! Continue following signs for "Holzbrücke." Walk over the bridge with Rapperswil in the distance. Follow signs to the Rapperswil Bahnhof, or walk through the Bahnhof and then through the city of Rapperswil, returning to the Bahnhof.

Trail Markers

Pfäffikon ≫ Hurden ≫ Holzsteg ≫ Rapperswil Bahnhof Süd

Tip

For those interested in touring the town of Rapperswil, walk through the train station and slowly meander through the quaint streets of this charming place. This is the perfect opportunity to purchase an ice cream and walk up to Rapperswil Castle, which dates back to the 13th century AD. Once at the top of the castle, there are incredible views of Lake Zurich and Obersee.

Special Features

+ Nature is plentiful.
+ The wooden footbridge is a unique and captivating aspect of this walk and is part of a UNESCO World Heritage Site identified as a "Prehistoric Pile Dwelling."
+ There is a playground at roughly 2 km into the hike.
+ Grilling is available at the playground. Firewood is also available.
+ Toilets are available at the playground and just before the start of the wooden bridge.
+ Rapperswil Castle is located at the end of the walk should participants elect to walk through the town of Rapperswil.

Be Aware

+ This is a stroller-friendly walk.
+ The trail is exposed and can be hot during sunny days. Bring plenty of water, hats, sunglasses, and sunscreen.
+ There are multiple fountains for filling water, but not until the town of Rapperswil.

Neu-Falkenstein Ruin ✕ 👥

Seblenhof Farm ★

Seblenhof Bus Stop 🚌

Start of Holzweg ★

/⊞\ playground　　🎪 picnic/grill spot　　👥 toilets

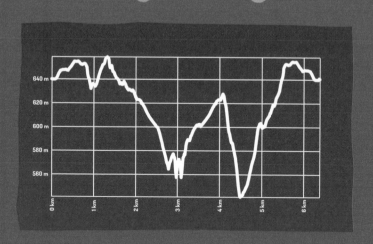

Holzweg Thal

Holderbank SO, Seblenhof
(bus stop)　　　　　　　　　　　　　　　　▷···

Holderbank SO, Seblenhof
(bus stop)　　　　　　　　　　　　　　　　···✗

4 h　　　　　　　　　　　　　　　　　　🕐

6.4 km

Spring through fall

Overview

This wood-themed trail located in the canton of Solothurn offers wooded trails, open meadows, and impressive views. The trail is one that families of all ages will enjoy. With interactive stations and art installations along the way, children will be anxious to walk to the next station. The views from the Neu-Falkenstein ruins are particularly beautiful.

The playground, located at the end of the hike, is a true haven for families, with climbing structures, a covered picnic table, two grilling areas, plenty of wood, and a toilet. Families will long to linger and enjoy this playful, well-thought-out area.

Directions

From the Selbenhof bus stop, pick up a copy of the "Holzweg Thal" information card from the small marked box. Follow the street (Seblenweg) up, passing a farm on your right and turn left at the crossroads. From that point, follow the yellow trail markers or the red sticks located along the base of the trail to continue on the "Holzweg." The trail will open up to a field and direct you towards "Ruine Neu-Falkenstein." This should not be missed as it is a large ruin offering expansive views over Balsthal and Weissenstein.

Return from the castle back through the field via which you came and then down the remainder of the "Holzweg." After the xylophone, the trail continues back up a hill leading to an amazing playground. This hike ends by returning to the Selbenhof bus stop.

Trail Markers

Seblenhof ≫ Stalden ≫ Ruine Neu-Falkenstein ≫ Alt Berg ≫ Plattenweg/Pavillon ≫ Seblenhof

Tip

Enjoy the gorgeous playground at the end of the hike and grill lunch while the children play.

Special Features

+ The hike starts almost immediately at a farm that has guinea pigs, rabbits, cows, goats, and donkeys.
+ This is a theme trail with interactive stations and art installations for the entire family to enjoy.
+ Plenty of grilling opportunities with wood supplied.

+ Benches along the way.
+ Neu-Falkenstein ruins, which offers 180-degree views.
+ Two toilets are available on the trail, one at the base of the Neu-Falkenstein ruins and the other at the playground.

Be Aware

+ This is not a stroller-friendly hike.
+ There are several sets of stairs to navigate at the castle.
+ There is no opportunity to fill up with water on this hike.
+ A bus takes you to and from this location with departures once per hour. Plan accordingly. Use caution when crossing the main road.

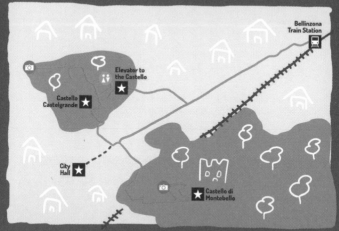

Bellinzona
Train Station

Elevator to
the Castello

Castello
Castelgrande

City
Hall

Castello di
Montebello

 viewpoint   toilets

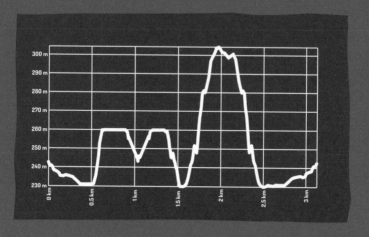

Bellinzona
Two-Castle Tour

Bellinzona
(train station)

Bellinzona
(train station)

1.5 h

3.1 km

Year round

Overview

This leisurely walk from the Bellinzona train station will take you through the picturesque town toward the impressive castles of Castelgrande and Montebello. There is also a third castle, Castello Sasso Corbaro, which is not part of this walk. All of the castles date back to the Middle Ages and are part of UNESCO World Heritage Sites.

Enjoy the relaxing vibe of the town center before making your way up to the dramatic castles, which will spark your children's imaginations. Start the walk up to Castelgrande, where families can enjoy the vast lawn areas and the surrounding views. After you have allotted enough time to enjoy Castelgrande, make your way back across town before climbing several sets of stairs to Montebello Castle. This walk is the ideal location to stop if families are moving on to Locarno or Ascona, providing remarkable views and ample time to stretch your legs.

Directions

Exit the Bellinzona train station and turn left down the main street (Viale Stazione). After 400 m, turn right onto Via Torre. This leads you to Piazza del Sole and along part of the castle wall at the end of which is a tunnel into the rock face. This tunnel leads to an elevator which will bring you up to Castelgrande. From the top of the elevator, turn right and continue into the castle noting the main entrance to your left. Explore the castle grounds and exit the main entrance. This path will meander down a broad walkway with some terraced steps, then narrow before depositing you adjacent to Piazza Collegiata. This area is worth a look, filled with cafés and beautiful architecture. To the right, approximately 90 m away, is the Palazzo Civico, the city hall with its picturesque courtyard. To the left is Piazza Collegiata, with the historically delicious Peverelli's Bakery and the Collegiate Church of Saints Peter and Stephen with its fantastic marble adornments. Continue along the small street to the right of the Church (Salita alla Motta), also indicated by a sign "Ai Castelli," which leads behind the Church. The path continues into a narrow walkway between houses, Salita Castello di Montebello. Continue up this narrow walkway as it zigzags and opens up to a hilly field at the base of Castello di Montebello. Once finished with exploring this castle, return down to Piazza Collegiata the way you came. As you enter the piazza, turn right, up Viale Stazione, which will take you back to the train station.

Tip

Stop at Peverelli's Bakery and pick up some delicious treats for the walk.

Special Features

+ The area is extremely picturesque.
+ Drinking water is available at Castelgrande and Montebello.
+ Food is available in the town center.

- ✦ Toilets are available at Castelgrande.
- ✦ There is an elevator that provides direct access to Castelgrande.
- ✦ Check opening times and special events offered by each castle at:
  www.bellinzonese-altoticino.ch

Be Aware

- ✦ This is not a stroller-friendly walk as there are stairs to navigate.
- ✦ Castles may not be open year round.
- ✦ Tours of Montebello Castle are available for five francs from mid-March to early November.

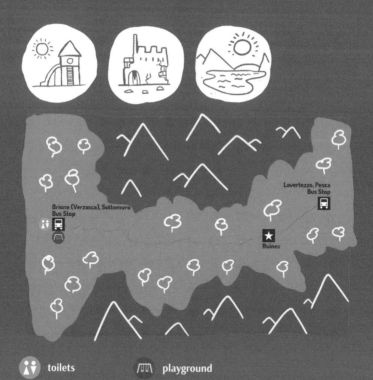

toilets

playground

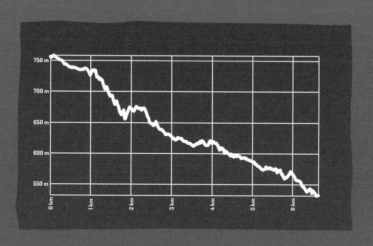

Val Verzasca
River Hike

Brione (Verzasca), Paese
(bus stop)

Lavertezzo, Paese
(bus stop)

3–4 h
(depending on stops)

6.7 km

Spring through fall

Overview

This scenic and memorable hike takes you along the gorgeous Verzasca River. With views of the transparent, turquoise water mixed with enchanted forests, families will take pleasure in the easy-to-navigate trail. With opportunities to drop down to the river and enjoy a picnic, families should pack a lunch and marvel at the surrounding nature.

At the conclusion of the hike, pull out your camera to capture the Ponte dei Salti (Bridge of Jumps), and on hot days, enjoy watching as people bathe in the cold river water.

Directions

Take bus 321 to the Brione (Verzasca), Paese bus stop. Once off the bus, you will notice a large playground across the street. This is a great place to let the kids play while getting ready for the hike. Behind the playground is an old church and a public toilet to the right. Start the walk by taking the driveway and walkway across from the playground past the walled-in building called "Trattoria di Castello." This places you in the middle of the old town surrounded by its gray stone houses. Turn left after the "Castello" followed by a right on Via Municipio, then left onto Via Passaroro, which returns you to Via Cantonale (the main road). This avoids the main road, which does not have a sidewalk along this section. At the main road, carefully cross and turn right. Continue along the sidewalk for approximately 200 m, then turn left onto a dirt road just after a bridge. Walk along the dirt road, around the football field, and across a small footbridge. Once through the parking lot, cross the large footbridge on your left. This crosses the Verzasca River. Turn right at the end of the bridge. This begins the main part of the hike along the river and through a forest of chestnut trees. After approximately 1.7 km, use caution crossing the main road and walk along it over the bridge, crossing to the other side of the river. Once across the river, the trail drops back into the forest at the end of a parking lot. The trail continues down river through small clusters of houses and ruins. In several locations the trail has spurs indicating White-Red-White hiking trails; the hike along the river is on a yellow trail and you will continue in the direction of Lavertezzo. Once you pass a small restaurant (Grotto al Ponte), the trail emerges just before the Ponte dei Salti where you can explore the stunning part of this river. Be mindful of the bus schedule and allow up to 10 minutes to walk across the bridge (Ponte dei Salti), down the river, and to the Lavertezzo, Paese bus stop, approximately 250 m from the bridge.

Trail Markers

Brione (Verzasca) ❯❯ Bivio Piee ❯❯ Ganne bus ❯❯ Ganne ❯❯ Piano ❯❯ Oviga ❯❯ Lavertezzo

Tip

Pack a towel, and perhaps bathing suits, to enjoy the river. Heed posted caution signs about river safety.

Special Features

+ The Verzasca River offers remarkable photo opportunities.
+ A playground is present at the start of the hike.
+ Toilets are available at the start of this hike.
+ There are a few water fountains available at the start of the hike.

Be Aware

+ This is not a stroller-friendly hike.
+ Though the river is gorgeous and enticing, use caution when wading or swimming. If children are in the water, keep them in close proximity. The temperature of the river is extremely cold, currents are likely, and the water has inherent dangers.

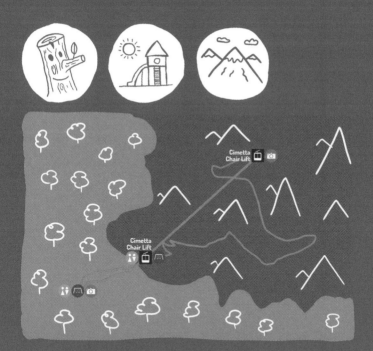

Cimetta Chair Lift

Cimetta Chair Lift

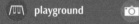 playground   viewpoint   toilets

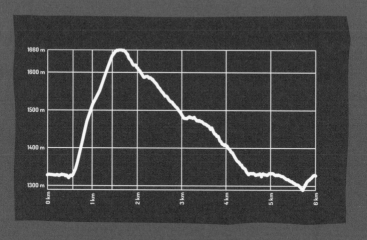

Cimetta Mountain Treasure Hunt

 37

Cardada
(cable car station)

Cardada
(cable car station)

4 h

6 km
(distance may vary depending on the route chosen)

June through October

Overview

The hike from Cardada to Cimetta is an interactive and child-friendly trail that allows you to choose your route based on the treasure hunt booklet available at the Cardada lift station. Children will be captivated immediately as they enjoy the barefoot trail, slack lines, and a play area located in the wooded section to the right of the Cardada lift station.

Families will be able to mark off the seven stations required to complete the treasure hunt and the corresponding animal footprints pictured on the sign postage. Once families finish exploring, hiking, and discovering, hand in your completed treasure hunt booklet at the bottom of the Cardada lift station to receive a small prize.

Directions

From Locarno take the Solduno Funicular up to the Orselina cable car station and continue up to the Cardada cable car station. (The Solduno Funicular is a private means of public transportation and the half-tax fare card and the Junior Travelcards are not valid, but bring the travel card provided by hotels for a 20% discount.)

Families will essentially be able to choose the route in which they complete the treasure hunt booklet, determining if they want to take the chair lift to the top of Cimetta mountain or walk up.

Tip

Consider making the hike a bit shorter and easier by taking the chair lift up to the top of Mount Cimetta and hiking down.

Special Features

+ Cardada is located at 1340 m and Cimetta is located at 1670 m.
+ This is a theme trail.
+ Playgrounds are located along the hike.
+ Water and food are available throughout the hike.
+ Toilet facilities are available along the hike.
+ For detailed information visit: *www.cardada.ch*

Be Aware

+ This is a White-Red-White trail.
+ This is not a stroller-friendly hike.
+ The Solduno Funicular from Locarno is cash-only.
+ Parts of this trail are steep should you elect to hike up to Cimetta.

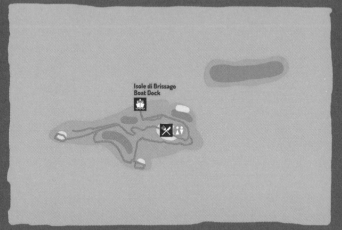

Isole di Brissago
Boat Dock

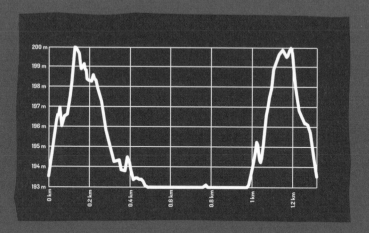 toilets

Brissago Islands Treasure Hunt

 38

Isole di Brissago
(boat dock)

Isole di Brissago
(boat dock)

2 h

1.5 km

Spring through fall

Overview

This enjoyable walk will captivate families from the moment they arrive by boat to the Brissago Islands. With lake and mountain views, the main island, San Pancrazio, is exciting and captivating. After paying the island entry fee, families should ask for the Brissago Islands Treasure Map and start their adventure.

The island is a gorgeous oasis of peace, tranquility, flowers, spices, and trees. Children will enjoy exploring the landscape, including the magical bamboo forest, and searching for items to stamp on the treasure hunt map. The area is a special place offering over 1,700 plant species, a hotel and restaurant, all with stunning views of Lake Maggiore.

Directions

Boats to the Brissago Islands are available from: Locarno, Ascona, Porto Ronco, and Brissago. At the boat dock make your way to the entrance where families will pay the entry fee and ask for the Brissago Islands Treasure Map. Allow the map to be your guide to the island as the children collect the 13 stamps required to receive their prize at the end of the walk. Families have the flexibility to choose the route they wish to follow.

Tip

Submit the Brissago Islands Treasure Map at the end of your visit to receive a small prize.

Special Features

+ For plant enthusiasts, the island is a remarkable sanctuary.
+ The island provides educational opportunities for families.
+ This is a theme trail.
+ There are toilets on the island.
+ A hotel and café are located on the island.
+ For opening times and detailed information regarding the Brissago Islands visit: *www.isolebrissago.ch*

Be Aware

+ This is a stroller-friendly hike but be prepared to put the stroller on the boat.
+ Be aware of the boat schedule.
+ The island's visiting hours are from 09:00 – 18:00.
+ Respect the plants and trees by staying on the designated trails.

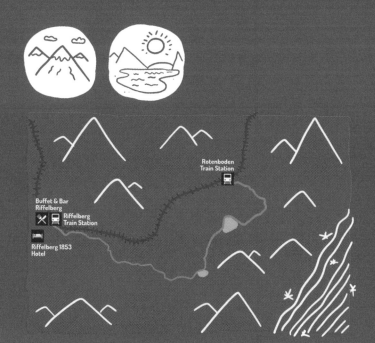

Rotenboden
Train Station

Buffet & Bar
Riffelberg

Riffelberg
Train Station

Riffelberg 1853
Hotel

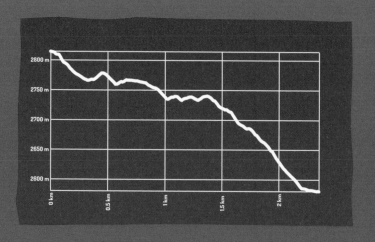

Rotenboden to Riffelberg

 39

Rotenboden
(train station)

▷•••

Riffelberg
(train station)

•••✗

2 h

🕐

2.4 km

Year round

Overview

When most individuals think of Switzerland, they naturally think of the iconic mountain peak, the Matterhorn, that straddles both Switzerland and Italy. With its triangular shape that juts out of the landscape, it is indeed impressive and worth a visit to marvel at its beauty.

This hike leads you from the Rotenboden Railway Station down to the Riffelberg Station and provides panoramic views of the Matterhorn and Weisshorn. This is a relatively easy hike, with the majority of the hike progressing downhill. Children will enjoy the scenic climb up the mountain by train and then welcome the opportunity to stretch their legs as they walk down the mountain.

Directions

Take the Gornergrat-Bahn from Zermatt to Rotenboden, one stop below Gornergrat. The trail begins on the left of the railway line (in the direction of the train heading downhill) and leads walkers down to Riffelsee and then continues down to Riffelberg where you can get back on the Gornergrat-Bahn and take the train back down the mountain to the village of Zermatt. Enjoy the stunning views!

Trail Markers

Rotenboden ≫ Riffelsee ≫ Riffelberg

Tip

In the winter, bring your sled! For stunning views on a clear day, the perfect family photo, and a good place to eat, take the Gornergrat-Bahn all the way to the top and exit at Gornergrat.

Special Features

+ Views of the Matterhorn on a clear day.
+ The historic Gornergrat-Bahn! Check the website prior to starting your hike: *www.gornergratbahn.ch*
+ Food and toilet available at the Riffelhaus 1853 hotel.
+ Great photo opportunities of the Matterhorn, Obergabelhorn, and Weisshorn.
+ Although the picturesque alpine village of Zermatt is not part of this hike, it is worth a visit.

Be Aware

+ This is a White-Red-White trail.
+ This is not a stroller-friendly hike; bring carriers for small children.
+ Be prepared with plenty of water and snacks.
+ This hike includes higher elevations; bring additional layers of clothing for changing temperatures and weather.
+ Check timetables for the Gornergrat Bahn, as they vary according to the season.

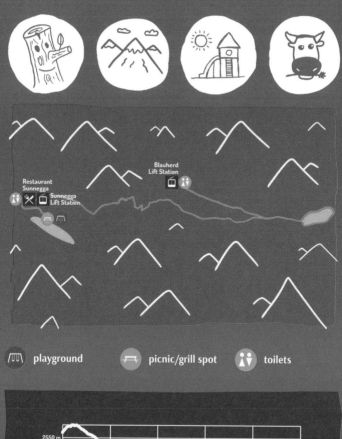

playground   picnic/grill spot   toilets

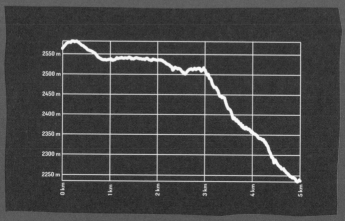

The Marmot Trail

Blauherd
(lift station)

Sunnegga
(lift station)

2 h

5 km
(with the Stellisee Loop)

June through September
Check snow levels and conditions with the local tourist office prior to starting out on this hike.

Overview

Zermatt is a special location, very touristy, but once on the trails, the crowds dissipate and the views are special. To skip Zermatt is to miss the true essence of Switzerland with the famous Matterhorn. The Marmot Trail offers not only an engaging theme trail for the family, but it provides quiet views of a captivating landscape. Enjoy the information signs along this route, take in the landscape and allow children to relish in their accomplishments as they play freely at the Wolli Adventure Park at Sunnegga. Be aware that this is a high alpine hike above 2400 m, which requires careful monitoring of children.

Directions

From the Blauherd lift station, exit and veer to the right. You will see a yellow trail marker indicating "Murmelweg." As the trail curves left, you will see the path before you at a shallow descent. At approximately 0.7 km, the "Murmelweg" trail switches back and continues to descend. Stop! We recommend continuing on the White-Red-White trail towards Stellisee (lake). On calm days, this lake offers great views with mountain reflections. Stop and take a family photo here! A loop around this lake is 1 km from the signpost. Once around the lake, continue on the "Murmelweg" towards Sunnegga. Just when you are below the Blauherd lift station, the sides of the trail become steep and additional switchbacks soon become visible. The trail at this point will open up with expanded views of the area. Prior to looking around, stop and consider harnessing your children at this point. After 1 km, the trail veers right around a mountain ridge and becomes less steep with the Sunnegga lift station visible in the distance. The Wolli Adventure Park at Sunnegga will be below the station. Follow the trail to the lift station and then to the lake. This is the ideal place to allow the children to run free and play or even spread out and have a picnic. The hike ends at the Sunnegga lift station.

Trail Markers

Blauherd >> Stellisee >> Sunnegga

Tip

Have your children stop and listen for the marmots. If they are able to hear their almost bird like sound or whistle, search for the animals in the landscape. Marmots call, or make the whistle sound to one another, especially if they are frightened. These animals hibernate in the winter months.

Special Features

+ This trail offers remarkable views throughout.
+ This theme trail offers information boards about the lives of marmots in English, German, French, and Japanese.
+ The trail ends at the beautiful and picturesque Wolli Adventure Park at Sunnegga.
+ Grilling opportunities are available at the Wolli Adventure Park at Sunnegga.

Be Aware

+ Parts of this trail are on a White-Red-White trail.
+ This is not a stroller-friendly hike; bring carriers for small children.
+ This hike is best suited for experienced hikers.
+ Never attempt this hike in poor weather conditions.
+ There are no toilet facilities along the route.
+ The hike offers no shade; bring plenty of water, sun hats, and sunscreen.
+ Harnesses may be used on this route.

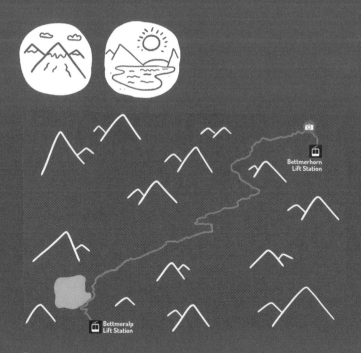

Bettmerhorn
Lift Station

Bettmeralp
Lift Station

📷 viewpoint

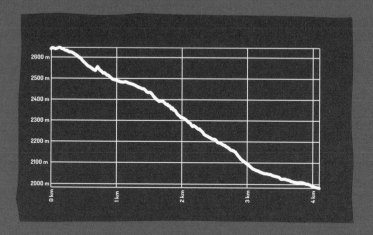

Bettmerhorn to Bettmersee

Bettmeralp (Bettmerhorn)
(lift station)

Bettmersee
(this is not a public transportation stop)

2.5 h

4.1 km

Summer through fall

Overview

From the top of the Bettmerhorn, you will take in the stunning and captivating views of the Aletsch Glacier, which is truly a sight to be seen. Enjoy the scenery at the top, take the perfect family photo, and then start this gorgeous hike. This particular hike offers striking views and interesting geology throughout. The trail does, however, have steep steps for little legs, requiring assistance at some points. About midway there is a zigzag section of the trail that requires you to step with care and to either harness children, or at the very least, have children move to the inside of the trail. This section is short, however, and with proper precautions, manageable.

Once finished with the hike, Bettmersee (lake) will appear, making the perfect spot to enjoy the water, take a swim, or walk over to the Sportzentrum Bachtla to enjoy further recreation.

Directions

Once off the gondola at the Bettmerhorn, from the glacier outlook, follow trail markers toward Bettmersee. The trail indicates 1 h 10 min but it will take families with children much longer. Follow signs to Hohbalm and veer left down the trail towards Bettmersee. The trail will continue turning right before a zigzag section. Use caution in this area. From this section the lake is in clear view with the trail running parallel to the gondola cableway. Continue on until the lake keeping an eye out for Sportzentrum Bachtla.

Trail Markers

Bettmerhorn ≫ Hohbalm ≫ Bettmersee

Tip

Take children to visit the free Glacier Museum at the top of the lift. Not only is it interesting, it's a phenomenal educational opportunity for the entire family. For those interested in searching for crystals, it may be possible to find some along the trail between the Bettmerhorn and Hohbalm.

Special Features

+ A photogenic hike with stunning views throughout and the expansive and impressive Aletsch Glacier at the start of the hike.
+ This is part of the UNESCO Swiss Alps Jungfrau-Aletsch World Heritage Site.
+ The start of the hike at the Bettmerhorn offers the World of Ice which provides a rich history of the Aletsch Glacier with free entry. This is the ideal opportunity to educate families on glaciers, global warming, and the impacts man has on the environment.
+ Children's play area at Sportzentrum Bachtla near the lake.

Be Aware

+ This is a White-Red-White trail.
+ An overnight in this area is recommended.
+ This is not a stroller-friendly hike; bring a soft-sided carrier.
+ Being a downhill hike, walking poles are helpful and advised.
+ There are big steps to navigate throughout which might be tricky for little legs.
+ The zigzag decent is open to sharp drops.
+ Hikers may experience drastic changes in temperature as the trail descends from 2647 m to 2009 m, so plan accordingly.
+ No opportunity to fill up with water once on the trail.

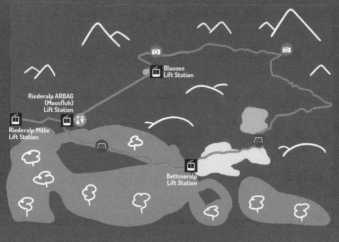

Riederalp ARBAG
(Moosfluh)
Lift Station

Riederalp Mitte
Lift Station

Blausee
Lift Station

Bettmeralp
Lift Station

🎠 playground   📷 viewpoint   🚻 toilets

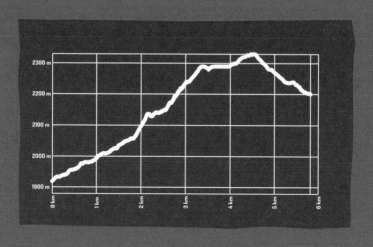

Bettmersee to Blausee

 42

Bettmeralp
(lift station)

Riederalp (Moosfluh)
(lift station)

3.5 h

5.8 km

Summer through fall

Overview

This hike is breathtaking and despite some uphill climbs, a true pleasure. Hikes like this are reminders of why living in Switzerland is such a joy. With views throughout and paths that eventually lead to the expansive and incredible Aletsch Glacier, the largest in continental Europe, one cannot help but wonder if this experience is really a dream. Once at Biel, the mountain crests and the views start to open up. Once over the small hill, the view of the glacier will be in sight throughout the entire walk to Moosfluh. The vastness of the glacier is impressive, as are the alpine flowers and small ponds. Once at Moosfluh, either take the gondola down or hike down to Blausee. After enjoying the lake, take the gondola from Blausee down to Riederalp; be aware that from the bottom of the lift station additional kilometers will be required to arrive at Bettmeralp (1.8 km) or Riederalp (0.7 km).

Directions

Exit the Bettmeralp lift station turning right on Bettmerstafel. After 350 m, veer left up the road at the Restaurant Panorama. Continue for another 200 m, taking a slight left (not all the way around the bend) uphill towards Bettmersee. After another 300 m you will see the Bettmeralp (Bettmerhorn) lift station on your right and you will turn left up to the lake on Donnerstafel. Once at Bettmersee, take the trail to your right at the edge of the lake. At the first intersection (150 m), veer right, away from the lake. At the second trail intersection/deviation keep left. The trail markers for Biel are no longer posted on the hiking signs; at this point follow the trail markers to Moosfluh. As the trail approaches the top and levels out, keep right (away from Moosfluh), this short deviation will reveal several small lakes with amazing reflections on a calm day and offers many rocks to sit on and have a picnic or a rest after the climb. Continue towards Moosfluh. At Moosfluh, take the lift down to Riederalp, or as we recommend, enjoy the panoramic descent (approximately 1 km) to Blausee, a picturesque small lake with its own gondola station. From Blausee, consider lunch at Bergrestaurant Chüestall or continue down to Riederalp from the Blausee lift station to end the hike. Connecting options from the bottom of the Riederalp (Moosfluh) lift station are either: return to Bettmeralp along the road (1.8 km) or go to the Riederalp Mitte lift station in the opposite direction (0.7 km).

Trail Markers

Bettmersee ≫ Biel ≫ Moosfluh ≫ Blausee *(option)*

Tip

Depending on the season, look in the small ponds just past Biel for tadpoles and frogs.

Special Features

+ Remarkable views of the Aletsch Glacier.
+ This is part of the UNESCO Swiss Alps Jungfrau-Aletsch World Heritage Site.
+ Incredible opportunities for photographers.
+ Plenty of nature to captivate children.
+ Wide, unobstructed views.
+ There is a play area at Bettmersee and another on the way from Riederalp/Moos-fluh lift station towards Bettmeralp.

Be Aware

+ This is a White-Red-White trail.
+ This is not a stroller-friendly hike.
+ Prepare to leave early in the day to allow plenty of time to complete the hike.
+ A good portion of the trail is uphill.
+ The trail is easy to navigate but does require a great deal of fitness, as hikers will go from 2006 m at Bettmersee up to 2333 m at Moosfluh.
+ Bergrestaurant Chüestall is located just below Blausee.
+ The Moosfluh area is being monitored for ground instability; all hikers should be aware and always check for trail closures to ensure safety. Contact the tourist office for more information: *www.aletscharena.ch*

 toilets

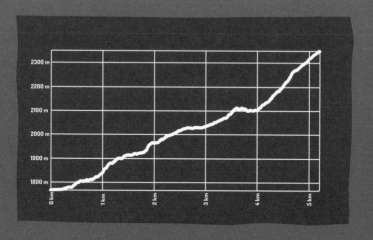

Fafleralp to Anenhütte

 43

Fafleralp
(bus stop)

Anenhütte
(this is not a public transportation stop)

3.5 h

5.2 km

Mid–June through October

Overview

The Lötschental Valley is an untouched and unspoiled area, surrounded by natural beauty. Void of crowds and tourists, rich with stunning views, the hike from the Fafleralp Post bus stop up to Anenhütte starts out relatively flat. With wild flowers in full bloom during June and early July, this hike begs you to walk slowly and take in the views. Pace yourself for the climbs until you reach the final destination of Anenhütte. Anenhütte is an exceptional destination but makes you earn your stay with a hearty climb all the way to the top. Though this hike is relatively short in distance, the terrain makes you labor to enjoy the stunning views available once at the top of Anenhütte. Anenhütte is a self-sufficient, off-grid hut set in a gorgeous location. To stay at the hut, reservations must be made in advance. This route (as an out-and-back hike) is too challenging to attempt in a day with children.

Directions

From the Fafleralp bus stop, follow the yellow trail markers in the direction of Anenhütte. This trail begins by heading through a campground and farm area. After approximately 200 m, the trail will divide. We recommend taking the left trail with children since it is easier and safer. The trail will begin to go into the forest; climb slightly above the river before climbing steeper through a mix of forest and tree stumps. At the next trail marker, keep right and continue up the trail through lush vegetation. The left and right trail will both lead to Anenhütte but the right trail is a bit shorter. From here, it is clear that this area may be subject to substantial snowfall and potential avalanches in the late winter months, which is indicated by the bent, broken, and felled trees.

There are two small sections of this trail that include steep edges; use harnesses for children or proceed with extra caution. The trail may cross a few snow patches (even in July), and then traverse a wide-open and flat landscape with lots of rocks before ascending back through more trees and flowering bushes. At this point the trail edge can become steep at times before arriving at a small gate (close the gate behind you) and bridge over an equally small gorge. Cross over the bridge continuing past the yellow trail marker towards Anenhütte/Anensee. The yellow trail becomes a White-Red-White alpine trail and will make the last climb up to Anenhütte. Be quiet and take the time to look up. There are ibex in this area, which can easily be scared by hikers with children. The ascending, zigzag trail is known as the "Lötschental Hanging Garden," due to the abundance of lush green landscape and flowers. Once the trail straightens, look for the natural spring that emanates right from the trail edge, approximately 0.5 km from Anenhütte. The last section of trail crosses through a small stream and wetland (which may be slick at times) from the run-off of Anensee, which is just a short walk away behind Anenhütte. For the return journey with children, it is best to follow this path in reverse.

Trail Markers

Fafleralp >> Anenhütte >> Anenhütte/Anensee

Tip

Anenhütte offers a geological kit for rent during your stay. Reserve this in advance and enjoy searching for crystals and special rocks on the trails behind the hut.

Special Features

+ There are amazing views of Langgletscher, which is part of the UNESCO Swiss Alps Jungfrau-Aletsch World Heritage Site.
+ Ibex can sometimes be spotted on the mountains. Enjoy searching with your children using binoculars.
+ Anenhütte, which is accessible by foot and helicopter, offers a cozy place to stay, delicious meals, and access to untouched nature. Secure your reservation in advance: *www.anenhuette.ch*

Be Aware

+ This is a White-Red-White trail.
+ This hike is not stroller-friendly.
+ Hiking poles may be useful for this route.
+ Snowfields may still be present during June and July, pass these sections with caution and assist small children.
+ There are large rocks throughout this hike, use caution and be aware of rock slides.
+ Never attempt this route during bad weather.
+ This trail has sections that are exposed and offer little shade. Plan accordingly and bring sunscreen, water, and sun hats for protection.
+ Water is only available just past the Fafleralp Post bus stop parking lot just as the hike begins. No other water sources are available during the hike.
+ Toilets are only available at Anenhütte and the Fafleralp Post bus stop parking lot.
+ There is limited to no cell reception inside Anenhütte due to the metallic cladding on the building, however, cell service is available outside (and away from) the hut.

Tracouet TDN
Lift Station

/ⅲ playground   picnic   👥 toilets

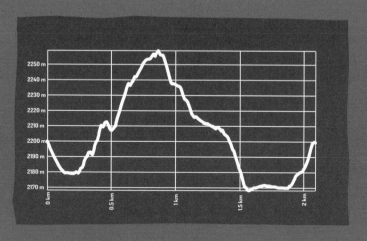

Panorama Trail

Tracouet (Haute-Nendaz)
(lift station)

Tracouet (Haute-Nendaz)
(lift station)

1.5 h

2.1 km

Summer

*To determine official trail openings, hours of operation, and gondola
schedules, please visit the official Nendaz website at: www.nendaz.ch*

Overview

This interactive, short theme trail holds children's attention as they search for pine cone seeds, observe avalanche structures, relax on an oversized bench, and attempt to cross the slack line. This trail offers stunning views throughout and a walk around the lake provides children with the opportunity to spot frogspawn, tadpoles, frogs, and alpine newts.

Directions

From the Tracouet lift station, head straight out keeping left and following the small sign post which shows a crow, Sentier Panoramique, and "par là." The start of the path is just past the small lake and marked by a small wooden archway/gate. The trail will zigzag up the hill through pine trees and then open up to a field offering expansive views above Nendaz and the Rhône Valley. The trail will continue to climb up and through a series of avalanche barriers and offers a large wooden lounge chair to relax. After a few switchbacks, the trail reveals a new expansive view to the west. The trail will begin to descend after a few stations and after a little more than halfway, there is a picnic area (station 7) with benches. As the trail continues to descend, great views are offered of the mountains to the south; look for Mont Blanc on a clear day and use the map at station 8 to help locate it! The trail will continue, crisscrossing yellow and White-Red-White trails (but all will lead to the lake), and then circle around the lake to the left where you can easily find your way back up to the lift station.

Trail Markers

Sentier Panoramique

Tip

Take your time at the lake and have your children search for alpine newts (an information board is part of the trail with pictures of these cool creatures). The newts love to feed on the frogspawn in the lake. In mid-July there are plenty to be found and they are visible from the shore of Lac de Tracouet.

Special Features

+ This is a theme trail designated by a crow and binoculars.
+ A toilet is available at the top at the lift station.
+ A playground is available at the Tracouet lift station.
+ On a clear day, it might be possible to view Mont Blanc in the distance (station 8).

Be Aware

+ This trail is a mix of Yellow and White-Red-White trail markers.
+ This is not a stroller-friendly hike.
+ Bring plenty of water as there are no opportunities to fill up along the route.
+ There are steep ascents to start off the hike.
+ Always check trail openings and gondola operating times before starting out on your hike.

Tourist
Information

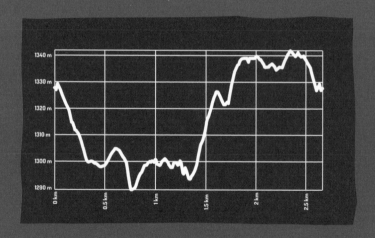

Sculpture Path

 45

**Nendaz Tourist Information Center/
Haute–Nendaz, station/poste**
(bus stop)

**Nendaz Tourist Information Center/
Haute–Nendaz, station/poste**
(bus stop)

1.5 h

2.7 km

Year round

Overview

The fun-for-families, easy-to-complete Sculpture Path takes hikers along a 2.8 km route where children are engaged throughout as they search for the 10 animal sculptures carved by Raphäel Pache.

Directions

From the Nendaz Tourist Information Center, turn right and cross the street (Route de la Station). Turn right again and continue down Route de la Station veering left after approximately 75 m onto Chemin du Cerisier. Be careful and watch your children at the end of this path as it connects again with the main road. Keep left, walking down Route de l'Antenne following the signs that point in the direction of "Promenade des Crêtes." The trail will continue along Route de l'Antenne and veer left approximately 0.8 km from the tourist office. This is where the sculptures can be found. Continue straight looking for the sculptures along the way. After approximately 1.5 km, the trail will switch back and head back to town along a dirt road, which will merge onto Chemin de Bermouche. After approximately 100 m, the trail will turn right (off the road) back onto a dirt path. This will merge on to Chemin des Crêtes and veer off of it (to the left) at the bend in the road. This path will zigzag through a parking lot and then back onto the main road in Nendaz. The tourist office will be in front of you, across the street.

Trail Markers

Promenade des Crêtes

Tip

Pick up the "Treasure Hunt" booklet for the Sculpture Path at the Nendaz Tourist Information Center. Once your children complete the booklet by answering questions along the Sculpture Path, return the booklet to the Nendaz Tourist Information Center to receive a special prize.

Special Features

+ This is a theme trail with 10 animal sculptures.
+ There is a treasure hunt along this route provided by the Nendaz Tourist Information Center.

Be Aware

+ This is not a stroller-friendly hike.
+ There are no toilets on this route.
+ Bring plenty of water as there are no opportunities to fill up along the route.
+ The first portion of this hike is on the road, proceed with caution and keep children close by.
+ Don't overshoot sculpture 1 as he could be hiding behind tree branches and overgrown bushes.

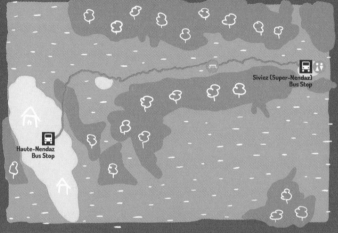

Siviez (Super-Nendaz) Bus Stop

Haute-Nendaz Bus Stop

👥 toilets   🏕 picnic

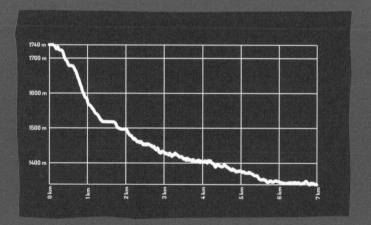

The Bisse du Milieu

Siviez (Super-Nendaz)
(bus stop)

Haute-Nendaz, station/poste
(bus stop)

4 h

7 km

Mid-May through mid-October
(for water to be present in the Bisse)

Overview

The Bisses of Valais date back to the 13th century and are irrigation systems that deliver water to the surrounding areas. The Bisse du Milieu in particular was created in the early 1700's and once provided energy for mills. This is a pleasant hike with ample shade. Children will enjoy following the waterway and wondering where it will appear next. The Bisse systems in Valais are very special; you may want to take the time to educate your family about the origin and the reason for the creation of the Bisses. To learn more about the Bisses of Valais visit: *www.les-bisses-du-valais.ch*

Directions

Once off the bus, head back in the direction the bus came from to the yellow trail markers (approximately 30 m from the stop). Cross the road and through the parking area of the Hotel Les Louerettes, veering right towards the small river. Proceed down the stairs and cross the bridge. Follow the trail markers to the left (towards Planchouet). The trail meanders along the La Printse River and then descends through forest and fields. Just before Planchouet, climb the fence or simply slide out the first railing for easier access and head down the field to a parking area which will be on your left. Continue straight along the road (Chemin de Planchouet) and then veer to the left at the trail markers to follow the Bisse du Milieu. Within 1 km, cross over the bridge and continue along the trail following the markers for Bisse du Milieu. Continue straight along the path with the Bisse exposed at your left for nearly the trail's entirety. After approximately 5 km, follow the yellow trail marker and proceed with caution across the road (Saclentse). Cross over to pick up the Bisse (a brown vertical sign labeled "Bisse" with a vertical squiggly line can be seen). Continue to follow the yellow trail markers which will lead across the road again at approximately 6.3 km, keep to the right and turn off the main road. The trail will briefly meander through a neighborhood and end at a fountain in the town of Nendaz. Continue down the street (Route de la Télécabine) approximately 200 m to the Haute-Nendaz, station/poste bus stop.

Trail Markers

Siviez ›› Planchouet ›› Le Bleusy ›› Haute-Nendaz

Tip

For an alternative and shorter route that will start almost directly on the Bisse du Milieu, take the bus to Haute-Nendaz, bif. Planchouet and follow the trail markers down the road Chemin de Planchouet to Bisse du Milieu. The total distance of the Bisse du Milieu is listed at 5 km and roughly 3 hours of walking time.

Special Features

+ This is a special Bisse hike.
+ Lots of shade throughout.
+ Enjoy a picnic at the designated area at La Printse or among the rocks along the Bisse.
+ There is a lovely designated spot to take a family photo near the end of the Bisse hike.

Be Aware

+ This is not a stroller-friendly hike.
+ There are no toilets on this route.
+ Bring plenty of water as there are no opportunities to fill up along the route.
+ The Bisse is not on public land and is privately held and thus must be protected and treated with respect by all observers.
+ Never throw anything into a Bisse.

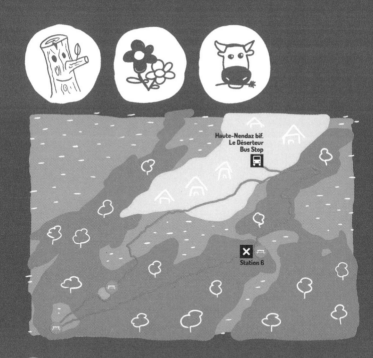

Haute-Nendaz bif.
Le Déserteur
Bus Stop

Station 6

 picnic

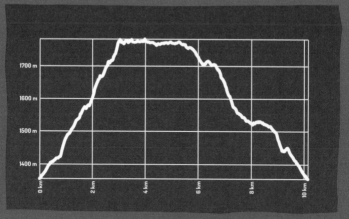

The Pine Cone Path and Bisse de Saxon

Haute-Nendaz bif. Le Déserteur
(bus stop)

Haute-Nendaz bif. Le Déserteur
(bus stop)

6 h
(with lots of stops and lunch)

10.1 km

Late May through mid-October
(for water to be present in the Bisse)

Overview

This theme path truly comes to life once you finish the uphill climb and reach station 6, which is the start of the Bisse de Saxon. After much effort, station 6 offers a picnic bench and the trail truly redeems itself with wide, flatter paths and many points of interest for the entire family to enjoy. The Bisse is a genuine delight for children and adults alike as are the many information boards providing details on the area. At station 8, the trail becomes even more interesting as it takes hikers over a stone wall path and very close to the Bisse itself. The Pine Cone Path is an all-day family event that treats families to lots of information, lovely forests and open views.

Directions

The trail starts at the Haute-Nendaz bif. Le Déserteur bus stop. A signpost is located between trees at the intersection and points up Route des Clèves. Follow the Sentier des Pives trail markers (wood with a green band and a pinecone). Continue up the hill passing a recycling station on your right, past the "Parcours" keep-fit trail (Zurich vitaparcours), and up the trail to the right at the 2nd station. This is a steep climb up. Turn right and continue along a road that crosses over the Bisse Vieux and then continue up the road. Once up the road (Chemin de Sofleu), past the 3rd station, and after the first bend, veer to the left onto a small trail to L'Étang de Sofleu (the Pond of Sofleu). This is the 4th station and a relaxing place to pause.

The trail then leads away from the pond and over the road; veer to the left and stay on the path and then continue up the hill through the woods, which switches back several times before arriving at the 5th station and then emerging onto a ski run. The last climb of the day is before you and in 400 m you will arrive at the Bisse de Saxon (station 6), where you can sit on a bench and relax to the sound of flowing water and enjoy a snack.

At the Bisse de Saxon, turn right to follow the Bisse. After crossing over a bridge (which also suspends the Bisse) you will arrive at station 7, which also provides a bench to rest. Continue along the Bisse and right after crossing a ski run, there will be a stone path and lichen-covered rocks at station 8; these rocks have been protected by the Canton of Valais since July 3, 2000. This area is very unique and the children may find the Legend of Dzèrjonne to be interesting as well. Walk carefully in this area, when it is damp you may find many small frogs along the path! Continue straight on the trail and when the tree canopy opens up to a wide field, you will notice a great photo opportunity. Follow the trail marker down the hill and have a picnic at Pra da Dzeu (station 10) if you haven't already. At the water fountain (in the field) go to the right through the grass field and down the hill back into the forest. The trail will soon lead past a picnic bench (on your right) and will arrive at station 11, Ouché Pond. When looking at station 11, continue on the path to the right, which leads around the Ouché Pond and reconnects with the main trail.

Follow the trail down the hill, station 12 will soon appear while the trail continues down the hill and to the right onto a road that crosses another road and becomes Chemin des Rairettes. The trail marker will then indicate to turn right and go up through a field and then past station 13. Continue straight along a road and look for the trail marker on the stone to the right. Following the trail markers, continue on Chemin du Torrent and along Route des Clèves down a steep, dusty path at the gondolas. Use caution in this section. Turn right on the path along the Bisse Vieux, which connects with Route des Clèves descending back to the start of the hike.

Trail Markers

Haute-Nendaz 》》 Sentier des Pives 》》 Les Rairettes 》》 Haute-Nendaz

Tip

Hang in there! The first five stations of this hike require up-hill climbs but at station 6 the trail comes to life with opportunities to picnic, a unique hike along the Bisse and the opportunity to search for tiny frogs depending on the season.

Special Features

+ This is a theme trail with 13 interactive information boards that educate you on trees, plants, legends from the area, and other interesting facts.
+ Part of this hike is along the Bisse de Saxon, which was constructed in 1876. It just so happens to be the longest Bisse in Valais running an impressive 26 km in length, though the Pine Cone Path takes you only along a portion of the Bisse de Saxon.

Be Aware

+ This local trail partially follows the yellow trail markers; you should always follow the wooden green signs with the pine cone.
+ This is not a stroller-friendly hike.
+ The first portion of this hike takes you on roads, proceed with caution and keep children close.
+ The first portion of this hike is uphill (just under 3km); prepare yourself in advance for this.
+ Prepare for a long day of hiking on this route. Pack a picnic lunch, drinks and snacks, and enjoy an entire day on the trail.
+ Bring plenty of water as there are no opportunities to fill up along the route.
+ There are no toilets on this route.
+ Bring bug spray.
+ The Bisses are not on public land and are privately held and thus must be protected and treated with respect by all observers.
+ Never throw anything into the Bisses.

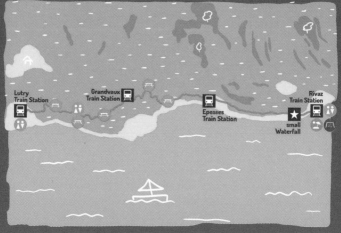

Lutry
Train Station

Grandvaux
Train Station

Epesses
Train Station

small
Waterfall

Rivaz
Train Station

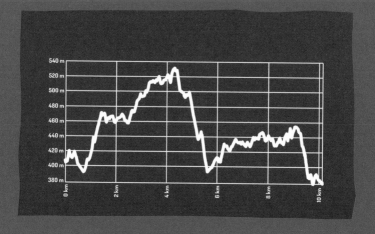

playground

beach

toilets

picnic

The Lavaux Vineyard Walk

 48

Lutry
(train station) ▷···

Rivaz
(train station) ···✕

---

4 h 🕐

10.1 km

Spring through fall 📅

Overview

This UNESCO World Heritage Site (designated in 2007) location is a winding route through the stunning Lavaux Vineyards. With exceptional views of Lake Geneva just in the distance, impressive mountain peaks and vineyards within reach, this walk is a genuine visual pleasure. Though this walk is long and exposed, it is such a treat to witness the scale of the vineyards, which literally grow right up to the edge of the train tracks and down to the lake. In the fall months, this hike is absolutely marvelous.

Directions

Exit the train station by track 1 and look for the yellow trail markers. Turn left (when your back is to the train station). Follow the green sign that says, "Terrasses de Lavaux." Do not follow the brown trail marker as it merely indicates a place to get information and is not part of the trail itself. Go up the stairs that cross over the train tracks, cross the street (Route de Savuit) and up a small stairway following the trail markers right onto Chemin de Bertholod. Go left at the yellow trail marker into the vineyards, turn right after 90 m, and another right after 70 m, then left at the bottom of the stairs along the train tracks. Go straight down to the road, cross over the road (Route Petite-Corniche) and follow the trail to the left up a small road. Stay on the road (use caution), crossing again over Route Petite-Corniche and then the first right onto Chemin de Chante-Merle.

Follow arrows straight into the vineyards. Continue straight through the town of Aran, turn right onto Rue de Village and follow the yellow trail marker "tourisme pédestre." Continue along, the trail markers will indicate a right onto Grand Rue. Once in the town of Grandvaux, follow the trail marker towards Chexbrex. Cross over the road (Route de la Petite Corniche) and up Sentier Grands Jardins and follow signs to Chexbrex. You will arrive in the town of Chenaux following the trail markers onto Chemin de Bahyse-Dessus. Use caution on this road. Follow the trail markers turning right onto Chemin du Carroz, then right onto a small path and down the hill before turning left onto Chemin de la Mouniaz. At the roundabout, turn left onto Route de la Corniche and through the town of Riex. Turn right onto Rue des Sous-Riez down the hill. At the bottom of the hill turn left, towards the town of Epesses, but before the town, keep right following signs to Rivaz/Terrasses de Lavaux. The trail will continue straight through the vineyards past historic places (Le Dézaley and Les Abbayes), following signs to Rivaz, and arrive at the train station or boat station in Rivaz, which will take about 20 minutes. To visit the beach, there is a walkway under the train tracks.

Trail Markers

Lutry ≫ Châtelard ≫ Grandvaux ≫ Epesses ≫ Les Abbayes ≫ Dézaley ≫ Rivaz
Also follow trail markers indicating "Terrasses de Lavaux"

228

Tip

This can be a rather long walk for children. It is possible to end in Grandvaux (3.5 km total), or end in Epesses (6.1 km total), although you will miss the beach in Rivaz. To help combat the fatigue we created a scavenger hunt exclusively for this walk (see final chapter). Simply grab the book and encourage your children to search for the items on the list. Oh, and don't forget to pick up a bottle of wine, or two, from the region. Enjoy the bottle with a fresh loaf of bread and some cheese. Bliss!

Special Features

+ This is a UNESCO World Heritage Site and an absolute stunning location.
+ There is a small waterfall on the way down to the Rivaz train station.
+ There is a water fountain available in Châtelard and a drinkable turn spout in the center of the fountain at Grandvaux. There are other water fountains along the hike but make sure the water is indicated as "eau potable" (drinking water).
+ There is a small stone beach located at the Rivaz train station with changing rooms, a shower, a small play area, and the opportunity to swim after a long walk. Enjoy this area.
+ The Lavaux Express Train is available. Reservations for specific routes are recommended: *www.lavauxexpress.ch*

Be Aware

+ This is not a stroller-friendly hike due to the numerous stairs that must be climbed and the uphill and meandering nature of the walk.
+ Parts of this walk are through streets and you must, at times, cross roads.
+ This hike offers little to no shade, making it extremely hot and exposed during sunny days and during the height of summer. It is not recommended on hot days, especially for children. Bring hats, sunglasses, and sunscreen.
+ Pack plenty of water and snacks.
+ There are no public toilets available on this hike, however, there is a public toilet at the Lutry train station.

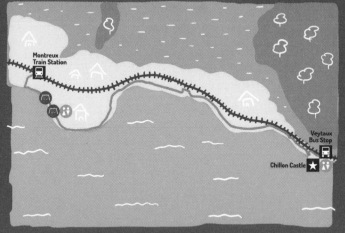

Montreux
Train Station

Veytaux
Bus Stop

Chillon Castle

 playground   toilets

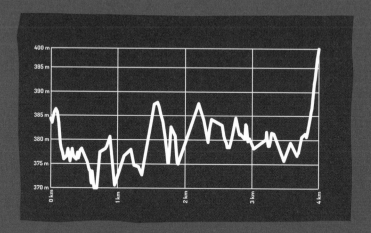

Chillon Castle Lake Walk

Veytaux, Château de Chillon
(bus stop)

Montreux
(train station)

1 h

3.9 km

Year round
Check the opening times of the castle: www.chillon.ch

Overview

This easy and relaxing stroll along the shores of Lake Geneva is a joy for the entire family. After a recommended visit to the impressive and historic Chillon Castle, walk slowly to thoroughly enjoy the views of the castle, the lake, and the vineyards. After sitting on one of the many available benches, or playing at a local play area, depart the area by train or boat.

Directions

After visiting the castle (with the castle to your back), turn left and follow the yellow trail markers towards Montreux, indicated as a one-hour walk to the boat or train station in Montreux. When starting out, stay straight but veer left onto and down the path by the railroad tracks and along the lake. Continue straight along the lake all the way to Montreux, approximately 150 m past the Montreux Ferry Terminal, then turn right at the flower garden, which will be on your right, and follow the trail marker up to the train station, perhaps the only trail in Switzerland with an escalator.

Trail Markers

Montreux Gare

Tip

This area is absolutely stunning with a genuine holiday feel. It is recommended to stay overnight in Vevey to make the most of the sights and walks that are available. Do not miss visiting the educational and impressive Chillon Castle which is open every day of the year except on January 1st and December 25th.

Special Features

+ This walk is beautiful and very easy.
+ Chillon Castle is photogenic; pack your camera.
+ Children will love the scavenger hunt pamphlet (Drako's Tour) distributed by Chillon Castle at the time of entry, making their castle experience that much more enjoyable.
+ Toilets are available at the castle and again at the old Market in Montreux.
+ A small play area, picnic benches, toilet, and a small kiosk with items for sale are located at 2 km into the walk.

Be Aware

+ This is a stroller-friendly walk.
+ Bring plenty of water for drinking.

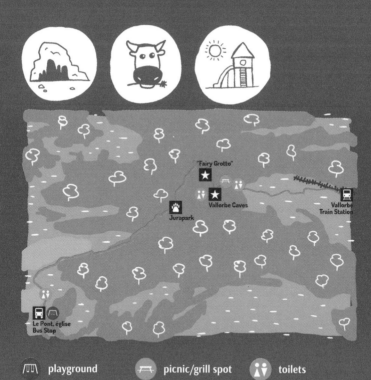

playground | **picnic/grill spot** | **toilets**

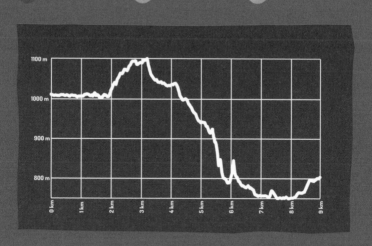

Lac de Joux to Vallorbe

Le Pont, église
(bus stop)

Vallorbe
(train station)

3 h

9 km

Spring through fall

Overview

The Lac de Joux and Vallorbe area is beautiful and offers an array of unique family activities. The Lac de Joux hike progresses through lush wooded areas and eventually along the boundary of the Jurapark. At the park, there are wild animals and a small petting area (across the road) with farm animals.

The second half of the hike provides another special opportunity to experience the local geology, as you hike down to, and into, the Vallorbe caves. The caves are impressive and not to be missed. It is quite possible your family will reflect on this memorable experience for days to come.

Directions

At the Le Pont, église bus stop (on the lake side of the street), you will see a playground. When facing the playground, turn right and continue along the lakefront ("Promenade romantique") towards the Le Pont train station. Cross the train tracks and take a quick right along the trail, which parallels the train tracks. This trail continues along Lac Brenet. At the end of the lake, turn right and cross the train tracks again, then veer right up the trail to the main road. Use caution and cross the road, turning left up the hill. Shortly after the trail goes into the forest, the yellow trail markers will point left and zigzag down a hill. The trail will continue along (but above) the road and then down, away from the road. The fence for the Jurapark will be visible, continue along the fence until the restaurant and entrance to the park.

After touring the park, the trail continues to your right (when facing the road from the restaurant). The trail will cross at the bend in the road; use caution. The trail will continue descending along a stone path through the woods. The trail will again cross the road, use further caution and listen for cars as the road curves in this area. The trail will continue through the forest until the trees become sparse and the trail widens. Though not marked, the trail switches back, turning right. The trail ascends to the road. Use caution at the road as this section means walking along the shoulder for approximately 200 m. The trail turns right and begins a steep descent that zigzags down to the river; approximately halfway down you will see a railing, at this point the trail has a spur (to the right), which will lead you to the "Fairy Grotto." At the railing, turn left to continue down the hill; keep to the right. This will lead you over a bridge to the Vallorbe cave entrance.

After touring the caves, continue along the trail, which follows the river downstream. At the parking lot, there are two directions to the train station; the recommended path on the right is more scenic along the river and points towards "Vallorbe centre 40 min," while the one to the left will take you along the road. Taking the right side leads up a road and around the power station. The path soon turns left into the forest and along the river. After a small zigzag in the trail, take the foot bridge across the river following the trail markers toward the Vallorbe train station.

Trail Markers

Le Pont >> Le Pont Gare >> La Torne >> Mont d'Orzeires >> Grottes de l'Orbe >> Vallorbe La Dernier >> Vallorbe Gare

Tip

If you are interested in exploring the "Fairy Grotto," it is best to bring a headlamp or torch/flashlight. This cave is just off the trail when descending from the road towards the Vallorbe caves and is approximately 120 m long, it may be intimidating for smaller children, however.

Special Features

+ There is a playground located near the Le Pont, église bus stop at the start of the hike.
+ More than halfway into this hike the Jurapark offers a nice break to observe animals (bears, bison, wolves, deer, goats, and alpacas). The café is also a good place to warm up on colder days.
+ Beautiful views of Lac de Joux and Lac Brenet.
+ The "Fairy Grotto" is a cave just off the trail. Be aware that this leads approximately 120 m into the mountain. Proceed with caution.
+ The 1 km underground walk through the Vallorbe cave takes you through impressive caverns. Allow 1–1.5 hours to enjoy the cave.
+ After touring the Vallorbe cave, the children will most likely want to buy a crystal at the entry kiosk and gift shop. Don't resist, it makes the walk to the train station more enjoyable.
+ Toilets are available at the start of the hike, at the Jurapark, at the Vallorbe cave entrance, and at the Vallorbe train station.

Be Aware

+ This hike is not stroller-friendly.
+ There are several road and train track crossings on this route; proceed with caution.
+ The Jurapark and Vallorbe caves require entry fees.
+ The Vallorbe caves are wet and cold. Wear appropriate clothes and shoes and watch your step as it is easy to get distracted looking up.

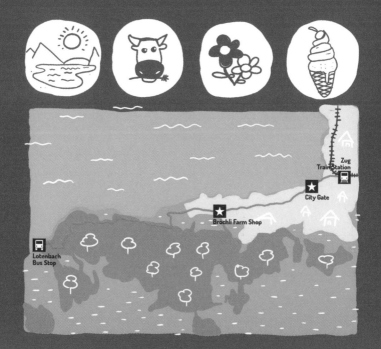

Zug
Train Station

City Gate

Bröchli Farm Shop

Lotenbach
Bus Stop

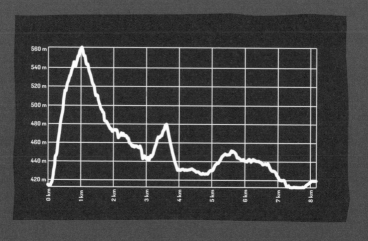

The Zug Cherry Blossom Hike

Walchwil, Lotenbach
(bus stop)

Zug
(train station)

4 h
(with plenty of stops)

8.2 km

Spring through fall
Summer is possible, though once out of the forest, the hike is on exposed paths, making the hike very hot with intense sun.

Overview

The first portion of this hike takes you up a steady climb for the first kilometer and through forests and then down wide-open paths. The hike is particularly enjoyable from the Bröchli Farm area, which is covered in blossoming cherry trees during the height of the spring. The farm offers a small honesty shop, which is the ideal place to stop and enjoy a fresh apple juice, coffee, and some seasonal farm goods. The hike ends in the picturesque town of Zug where a bird aviary will capture the children's attention, as will the expansive lake with snow-covered peaks in the background. Once at the lake, purchase an ice cream, find a shady spot, and enjoy the views. From the lake area it is roughly a 10-minute walk back to the main train station in Zug.

Directions

From the Zug train station, board bus number 5 towards Walchwil. Exit the bus at the Walchwil, Lotenbach bus stop and watch for bikes when getting off the bus. The trail starts at the crosswalk behind the bus. The trail will continue to the left after crossing the street and begins an uphill climb for roughly 1 km and offers expansive views of Zugersee, Mount Rigi, and Pilatus. The trail will split; follow the trail left (over a bridge) towards Zug. After the trail exits the forest, there will be a steady and manageable downhill section, keeping right on Weidlistrasse, which will go uphill. The trail will continue to Zug Oberwil and past Zug Oberwil train station. Just around the corner, as the trail curves right, is the Bröchli farm shop where you can stop for a snack. Continue past the cherry orchards and into the streets of Zug. From there follow signs to "Casino," though continue past the "Casino" train station and follow signs to "Altstadt" or the old city. At this point, meander through the impressive small town along the lake. The main Zug train station is a 10-minute walk from the lake boat dock.

Trail Markers

Lotenbach ≫ Hasal ≫ Rebmatt ≫ Zug

Tip

Complete this hike when the cherry blossoms are in full bloom (typically the first two weeks in April) to take full advantage of this beautiful and picturesque area. The Zug Tourism website also offers a "cherry bloom hotline," which can be called to determine if the cherry trees are at their peak by calling +41 (0)41 723 68 00 or emailing: *info@zug.ch*

Special Features

+ The trail starts in the forest providing shade and cooler temperatures during hot days.
+ The majority of the path is wide and easy to navigate.
+ There are views of the lake, Mount Rigi, and Pilatus throughout the hike.
+ There is a grilling area with a picnic bench just past Hasal.
+ There are multiple benches along the route, which allow for ample time to rest.
+ The cherry trees at the "Bröchli Hofladen" farm are amazing during the spring.
+ There is a small farm shop with fresh items (apple juice, coffee, ice cream, milk, and eggs) available for purchase by the honor system at the "Bröchli Hofladen" farm.
+ The farm also has chickens and goats for the children to observe.

Be Aware

+ This is not a stroller-friendly hike.
+ There are no water stations until the town of Zug.
+ There are no toilet facilities so it is recommended to use the toilet on the train before boarding the bus.
+ Half of the trail is exposed and provides little to no shade. Plan accordingly during hot days.

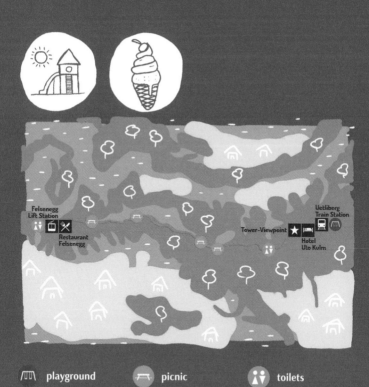

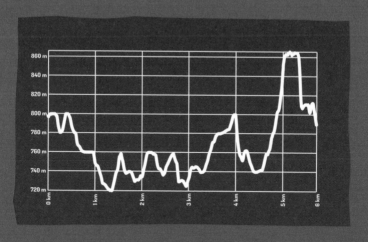

/ᐯᐯᐯ\ playground   🪑 picnic   👫 toilets

Felsenegg to Uetliberg (Panorama Trail)

 52

Felsenegg
(lift station)

Uetliberg
(train station)

---

2 h

---

6 km

Year round

Overview

This easy hike on Zurich's mountain, the Uetliberg, offers the perfect opportunity to spend a relaxing Sunday in the woods, away from the frenzy of city life. With expansive views of Zurich throughout, this is an ideal hiking point. The quick and efficient ride up to Felsenegg from the Adliswil Cable Car provides a relaxing city escape throughout the year. With a playground at the start and end of the hike, this is a leisurely excursion.

Directions

From the Felsenegg lift station, walk straight into the woods following the signs to "Uetliberg 1 h 35 min." Continue straight on the path. Do not follow the "Planetenweg" trail markers which will intersect and overlap in Balderen. Continue on to Uetliberg Kulm for 360° views of Zurich and then continue on to the Uetliberg train station.

Trail Markers

Felsenegg ≫ Balderen ≫ Folenweid ≫ Uetliberg

Tip

For CHF 2 climb the Uetliberg observation tower for impressive views of the area.

Special Features

+ There are multiple lookout points along this route.
+ This hike overlaps a portion of the Planetenweg trail.
+ There is a playground at Felsenegg and again at the Uetliberg train station.
+ There are several water sources along the route.
+ There are several restaurants along the route providing food and beverages.
+ There are multiple grilling stations along the route. Pack a lunch.
+ Toilets are available at the Felsenegg lift station and again just before the uphill section to the Uetliberg.

Be Aware

+ This is a stroller-friendly hike. There are stairs heading up to Uetliberg Kulm, however, you can continue along the trail arriving at Uetliberg Kulm from the other side which does not have stairs.
+ Bikers frequent this trail. Use caution with small children and remember to share the trail.
+ This is a popular destination/route.

CHAPTER IV

Happy Trail Kids

"

Time spent playing with children is never wasted.

"

DAWN LANTERO
AUTHOR

Welcome to chapter 4 and congratulations on making it this far! Our hope is that you have discovered this chapter before starting your first hike or completing your 52nd adventure, because the pages that follow were designed to put smiles on faces, decrease meltdowns, and insert a bit of trail magic along the way.

In this chapter, you will discover ways to stimulate family conversations on the trail, encourage playfulness, and teach a number of transferable life lessons. The activities will allow children to cover more distance while being fully immersed in their surroundings.

Some of the activities are designed to be completed by children on their own (labeled with the "kids" icon), whereas others (labeled with the "parent" icon) may require a bit of assistance, initiation, or equipment from adults, but we encourage everyone to take part in the tasks regardless of their size.

Parents

Kids

May this section of the book ignite children's curiosity, all the while teaching fortitude as children continue to place one foot in front of the other until the final destination is reached. Keep in mind, however, that it isn't so much the end point that matters, but the joy you experience along the way.

Now it is time to start the journey, collecting memories and kilometers under your feet.

Conversation Starters on the Trail

These conversation starters are for both parents and children. Take turns asking your child questions and then hand them the questions and encourage your child to ask you some as well. This is the ideal opportunity to have honest conversations while on the trail.

+ If you had one superpower what would it be and why?
+ If you could eat anything you wanted for breakfast, lunch, and dinner, what would your menu look like?
+ If you had 1 million dollars, what would you do with it?
+ If you could have any pet you wanted (regardless of size) what would it be?
+ If you could make a movie, what would it be about, who would be in it, where would it take place, etc.?
+ What is your favorite food? Could you eat that food for one meal every day for the rest of your life?
+ What would you like to invent? Why?
+ If you could create a new holiday, what would you celebrate? What date would the holiday take place and what would be some of the traditions celebrated on your special day?
+ What would your ultimate party look like? Who would you invite? What would you eat? Would there be games, music, animals, and entertainment? Where would the party take place?
+ What does kindness mean to you?
+ What do you hope to be when you grow up? Why?
+ Who do you admire and why?
+ Do you have a hero? If so, who is your hero and why?
+ What is your favorite book and why?
+ If you could have dinner with anyone in the world, who would it be and why?
+ What do you think would be the best job in the world? Would you want that to be your life's work?
+ Is it ever OK to break a rule? If yes, then when would it be OK to break one?
+ What is one problem in the world you would like to solve?
+ If you could create your own trail name (a name people call you while hiking), what would it be and why?
+ What is your family mascot (animal, or object that represents your family)?
+ If you were told you could only bring one tool, one meal, and one personal item (not a person) to a remote island, what would you bring and why?

Would you rather...

+ ...swim all day, or hike all day?
+ ...live simply or with lots of possessions? Why?
+ ...wear your shirt or your pants on backwards?
+ ...live in the mountains or by the ocean?
+ ...go to space or visit the deepest part of the ocean?
+ ...eat fruits only or vegetables only for the rest of your life?
+ ...be a child forever or a grown-up forever?
+ ...bike everywhere or skateboard everywhere?
+ ...own a dog or a cat?
+ ...live on a farm or in a city?
+ ...fly everywhere or take a train everywhere?
+ ...celebrate your birthday or your favorite holiday every day for one year? Why?
+ ...it be summer or winter all year?
+ ...have a cow as a pet or a donkey?
+ ...go to school every day or go to work every day?
+ ...color your hair bright pink or shave your head?

Survival questions: How would you...

+ ...build a raft?
+ ...start a fire?
+ ...create a shelter?
+ ...find drinking water?
+ ...call for help?
+ ...stay warm?
+ ...find food?

Instant Mood Lifters

There will be times while hiking that you, as the parent, might just wish you had stayed at home for a multitude of reasons. It's normal and it happens to us all. When this occurs, take the time to be grateful and recognize all the beauty that surrounds you. Ask each person in your group to state three things they find special about the area, and/or that they are grateful for. Notice the mood lift. If that doesn't seem to work there are more options listed below that you can pull out when times get tough. Just remember to laugh off the difficult times and, believe it or not, you are creating awesome memories for your child.

Have you ever blown bubbles for your child and watched as the mood changes? To keep children entertained along any trail and once you are in a flat, safe section of the route, blow bubbles and see how many your child can catch or count. Take turns seeing who can blow the biggest bubble.

Follow the leader. Each person in the group can take turns leading the hike. Stay on the trail and know your final destination. Children will feel empowered and happy to take charge.

Search for the tiniest creatures along the trail and hidden treasures all around you. When hiking, we often focus our gaze forward, but take the time to look up (carefully, however, still paying close attention to the trail). What do you see? One time we spotted a cluster of bright yellow mushrooms growing high up on a tree trunk. Another time we spotted whimsical tree houses in the forest. Also look down when walking. When you take the time to look where your feet step, you might just discover tiny wonders on the trail. For example, little frogs, salamanders, and rocks with unique shapes.

Play a game of "I Spy." Ask for a volunteer to start the game by saying for example, "I spy a squirrel." The group is then responsible for finding the squirrel. Whoever finds the squirrel first gets to start the next round.

Be silly. Encourage your child to look for animal poop along the trail. As gross as it may sound to the adults, children always giggle whenever they hear the word "poop." Despite the revolting subject matter, turn it into an educational game by trying to identify which animal created such output. The most common poop sightings may include: cow, horse, dog, sheep, and goat.

Take a break, eat a snack and/or whittle a stick. This is the perfect time to pull out that special treat you packed or purchased along the way.

15 Awesome Outdoor Activities

1. Play the cloud game. Take turns spotting shapes, letters, animals, etc. in the clouds.

2. Play the ABC game. Start with a word that you see on the trail that begins with the letter A, then B, then C, taking turns with family or friends. Go all the way until you reach the end of the alphabet. If a person cannot think or find something that begins with the letter, they are out of the game.

3. Take your favorite poem and read to the group when you are on the trail having a break. Also take turns creating your own poem. If you need inspiration, rhyming poems are typically the easiest to create.

4. Sing the verse to a song everyone in the group knows. Once the person stops singing, they must call on another person to finish the lyric. For example, "Row, row, row your boat, gently down the... Anne!" Anne must now finish the verse by saying, "...stream, merrily, merrily, merrily, merrily life is but a dream." If they are able to successfully complete the verse, they choose the next song to sing.

5. Try to build a mini cairn along the trail with the smallest rocks you can find.

6. Search for Swiss flags on the trail. How many flags can you count along your route?

7. Create trail names for yourself, friends, or family. Here are a few fun names to get you started: Trail Blitzer, Baby Foxy, Granola Gal, Chocolate Runner, and Muesli Mama.

8. See how many different flowers you can spot on the trail. Draw those flowers or take pictures to insert later into a nature journal that will help you record your findings.

9. Pick up rocks and get them wet. Discover the colors that appear once they are wet.

10. Take a picture of a new discovery on the trail.

11. Try to skim stones on a river or a lake. Who in your group can skip one stone the most times?

12. Make a grass whistle by placing a blade of grass in between your two thumbs and blowing. It is not easy, but if you get it to work, it will make a loud noise.

13. Play a game of tic-tac-toe in the dirt while enjoying a break.

14. Play the animal game. One person thinks of an animal and provides clues about that animal to the group, which then tries to guess which animal the person has in mind.

15. Do not forget to bring along a pair of binoculars or create your own using toilet paper rolls and string. Look for animals, flowers, or the moon in the distance. If you make your own binoculars, have fun decorating them.

Why Do Cows Wear Bells?

If you have ever been walking in the mountains, you cannot help but hear all those cowbells ringing in the distance. But the big question is, why do cows wear them? We recently asked a farmer/cheesemaker the same question and she responded with two very interesting answers.

1. The cowbells help farmers find their cows, especially in foggy or poor weather conditions. By listening for the bells, they have a better idea as to where their cows are grazing. Remember, cows need to be milked twice per day, so as a farmer, bringing them back to the barn on time both in the morning and in the evening is very important.

2. Cows are herd animals, which means they naturally group themselves together for social interaction and safety. When a cow strays from the herd, the ringing of the bell assists the animal in returning to the group, where they feel most secure.

Now that you know why cows wear bells, listen for them on your next hike. Don't be shy when it comes to asking farmers in the Alps questions about animals and farming. They will more than likely be happy to answer your questions.

The Cow Bell Challenge

How many cowbells can you count while you are on the trail? Who in your group can find the biggest bell? Who can find the smallest bell? Remember, bells are not only worn by cows; look for bells on other animals too. You may even see cow bells decorating a barn, so look around and see what you discover.

Nature Scavenger Hunt

When you are on the trail, see how many of the items you can find below.

○ A dog on the trail

○ Snow

○ A rock in the shape of a heart

○ A butterfly with white wings

○ Moss growing somewhere

○ A person laughing

○ A cow

○ Water running

○ A purple flower

○ A brown leaf

○ A bird singing

○ A white stone

○ A pinecone

○ A Swiss flag

○ A piece of
wood

○ A cloud in a
special shape

○ Something
blue

○ A water droplet
on a leaf

○ A piece of trash that must
be thrown away

Lavaux Vineyard Scavenger Hunt

This scavenger hunt is intended for the Lavaux Vineyard Walk *(hike no. 48)*.
See how many of these items you can find along the way!

O One helicopter
(these are typically
crop dusters)

O Four red triangular
field markers

O Eight
red leaves

O Five water
fountains, though
they may not all be
used for drinking
water

O Five boats
on the lake

O A pink flower

O Six trees

What is the color of the grapes you see growing?

_____

○ The phrase: "There's no better place and time than here and now."

○ Two places to picnic

○ A train

○ Ten houses

○ A lizard that spits water out of its mouth

How many wine barrels can you count along the route?

_____

○ Can you find "1998" along the route?

○ Nine cars

Lizards. How many can you count?

_____

○ Seven staircases

○ Three yellow triangular field markers

Reading Maps

Parents, we encourage you to teach your child how to read a map and allow them the opportunity to navigate while on the trail. Once your child understands the importance of navigational skills, allow them to complete the map challenge on their own.

Maps are important resources created by professionals called cartographers. Maps help us navigate, let us know where we are, and help us determine where we want to go. People have been using maps for thousands of years.

There are different types of maps that each serve unique purposes. For hiking, the maps most often used are physical maps, representing the physical elements of a country or area. These maps typically include: land, water, and mountains.

Topographical maps use a series of parallel curves to show the elevation changes and the features of the landscape. Curves coming closer together indicate steep hills and/or mountain areas, whereas curves that are farther apart tend to represent shallow slopes or flat areas. These types of maps also show specific points to aid in their navigational use, such as a point, cross, or triangle accompanied by a number to indicate a peak and its elevation. The maps also show boundaries, forests, and exposed rock or scree, among other important features to help navigate.

There is typically a map for each hiking area in Switzerland. These maps are often available at Tourist Information Centers, gondola stations, train stations, and sometimes even at the hotel or mountain hut where you are staying. Keep in mind that some of the free maps may not contain details and are not as accurate as a topographical map. Obtain a map and keep it on you as a reference guide and for safety purposes.

There are important symbols on maps that help you understand them better. Each map should have what is called a "key" or a "legend." The keys or legends will help you unlock the mystery of the map by using symbols, icons, and/or pictures to indicate important points of reference.

Take a good look at your hiking map and look for letters, colored lines, and symbols. Each one has a job to do: to highlight a point of interest located along a particular route.

Listed below are some symbols that you might see on your map and what they mean, however, not all symbols/colors are universal.

+ Different icons showing modes of transportation.
+ Colored lines – those imply the type of trails that are in the area. For example, a red line may indicate a hiking trail. A dotted red line might indicate a mountain/alpine hiking trail. An orange line might specify a biking trail.
+ There are symbols that indicate lookout points.
+ An icon of a bed shows a hotel or a place to stay for the night.
+ A fork and a knife indicate a place to eat.
+ A black triangle stipulates a place to camp.
+ A shopping cart specifies a place to purchase food and/or groceries.
+ An icon of a fire stipulates a place to grill.
+ A white "i" on a blue background indicates an information location.
+ The map will also contain the mountain peaks in the area including their height in meters. This way, when you are hiking and look up at a mountain in the distance, you will be able to identify which mountain you see, which can help you determine your location and/or serve as a point of reference for navigation.
+ The blue bodies of water are lakes. Their names are also included.
+ Some maps will even list the timetables for public transportation, as well as suggested hiking or biking routes in the area.

Map Challenge

Now that you know how to read a map, and some of the important symbols to look for, you are ready to test your map-reading skills.

With your map in hand find the following:

+ Point to your current position on the map.
+ Point to the direction in which you are headed.
+ Is there a place to sleep along the route?
+ How will you get back to your start location once you reach the end of your hike? Is there a form of transportation for you to take? Will you walk back?
+ What type of trail will you be hiking on?
+ Where will you be able to get food along the route?
+ Will you come across a lake?
+ Will you be able to grill your lunch somewhere on the way?
+ What is the highest mountain you will see during your hike?

Tip for parents
Secondhand stores, such as a Brocki, are perfect locations to find older maps. These maps may provide details on how the landscape of a particular area once looked and can still be used in most cases. These maps also make incredible souvenirs.

How to Use a Compass

Navigating by compass is not only a valuable life skill, it is also a fun way to navigate trails.

A compass is a tool used to help individuals navigate and orient themselves. Some people who rely on compasses are: sailors, pilots, search-and-rescue teams, and backcountry guides.

There are four main directions on a compass: North, South, East and West. However, the points in between these four points are referenced as: Northeast, Northwest, Southeast, and Southwest. Remember, the sun rises in the East and sets in the West regardless of where you are in the world (except the Poles!).

A compass will always point to magnetic North. A compass works because the Earth is one giant magnet, which is why the compass will point North with its magnetized needle.

Compass Challenge

With the skills to navigate using a compass, you must now figure out the following based on the image of the children on the map as a point of reference:

Which direction is:
the playground, the Berghaus, the gondola station, and the ice cream stand?

Where in Switzerland?

The next time you are at a Swiss train station, pick up the free "Swiss Travel System Map." Why would you want to do this? With the map in your hands, you can complete the three tasks below to become more familiar with Switzerland.

Task Number 1
Find and circle on the map where you are currently going.

Task Number 2
Circle all of the places in Switzerland you have visited.

Task Number 3
Highlight on the map all the places you would like to visit.

Hold on to your map so that you can track all of the places you continue to visit in Switzerland.

Be an Environmental Hero

We can all make small choices each day that will have a large impact on the environment. Here are a few ways that we can all make a big difference. Remember, this is not a full list, so get creative and come up with your own ideas for making our planet not only beautiful, but healthier as well. Share these ideas with your family and friends.

✦ Recycle paper, plastic, glass, and aluminum.
✦ If you see trash on a trail while hiking, pick it up and place it in its proper place. You can bring a small bag to place trash in and gloves to keep your hands clean.
✦ Reduce the amount of plastic you use. Though plastic has been a helpful resource in some regards, there is simply too much in the world, which is causing major problems in our oceans, for the wildlife, and our water sources. Ways to reduce plastic include: bring your own bags to all stores, reuse utensils, carry refillable water bottles, and limit the amount of food in plastic you purchase.
✦ Try not to purchase new items such as toys and clothes. If you have friends or family members, ask them to share their clothes that no longer fit or toys they no longer use. Also, consider trading your things with your friends.
✦ Plant a tree or even a garden.
✦ Use public transportation, which in Switzerland is very easy to do.
✦ Don't waste water and consider taking shorter showers.
✦ Turn off the lights whenever you leave a room.
✦ Eat local fruits and vegetables.
✦ Cook fresh meals.
✦ Remember that Earth Day is celebrated around the world each year on April 22nd. Earth Day was created in 1970 as a way to help create awareness regarding those issues that currently affect the environment. Earth Day encourages people of all ages to take action when it comes to cleaning up and protecting our planet.

Increasing Outdoor Time

Getting your child outside shouldn't be a chore; in fact, it should be a true pleasure. If you are looking for ways to increase your outdoor time as a family, besides hiking, consider the following:

+ Teaching your children to take photos of nature and create a photo journal of their experiences.
+ Having a scavenger hunt on a trail.
+ Encouraging your children to draw the flowers, stones, trees, or insects that they discover and keep their artwork in a nature journal.
+ Inviting some friends for an afternoon of grilling in nature.
+ Participating in a full moon walk.
+ Choosing a day for you and your children to clean up the Earth: putting garbage in its proper place, clearing debris from beaches, and learning the importance of properly disposing of trash.
+ Picking seasonal fruit and vegetables with your children. There are multiple farms around Switzerland that encourage us to observe nature and its bounty.
+ Observing seasonal changes with your family prompting your children to think about transformations and witnessing firsthand how they impact plants, trees, animals, and people.
+ Joining or creating a local scouting group.
+ Learning with your children how to identify and smell fragrant plants/flowers, such as: lavender, butterfly bushes, honeysuckle, and roses.
+ Scheduling a vacation in nature. Even without hiking you can visit the mountains, a lake, and/or a beach and spend your holidays getting the most from the natural world.
+ Creating a family challenge, 15 hours of fresh air in one week, for example. Once you have accomplished that goal, set a loftier one and work together as a family to achieve the task.
+ Trying an overnight camping trip, with a campfire and stories.
+ Signing up for a forest playgroup or forest camp.
+ Holding a play date in a local forest.
+ Planting a garden with your children; this is possible even if you live in an apartment and have a small balcony. Consider planting tomatoes, peppers and/or strawberries.
+ Hanging a bird feeder and watching the birds delight in your generosity. Encourage your children to try and identify the birds they see.
+ Taking your children to a local composting site and explaining the process.
+ Visiting a botanical garden periodically throughout the year.

+ Watching the stars at night and trying to identify planets and constellations with your children. There are multiple apps to assist with this experience.
+ Taking your children to recycle and teaching them the importance of not throwing away items that can be recycled or reused.
+ Taking story time outdoors. Pack your favorite books and spread out on a comfortable blanket and read. It doesn't have to be a destination – read in your back garden, on the balcony, or at a local park.
+ Playing games outside. For example, blindfold your child and hand them objects found only in nature. The child has to rely on their sense of smell, touch, sound, and/or taste to identify the objects handed to them.
+ Taking a day trip to a butterfly garden, botanical garden, farm, or animal park.

Creating Memories

For parents
If you are looking for a creative way to remember your travels, consider purchasing a postcard in each destination you visit for your child. Write something memorable about your trip, what you ate, and perhaps funny moments. Date the postcard and write your child's name on the card. Give these to your child when they get older as a reminder of all the travels that they experienced during their childhood.

For children
With the help of your parents, purchase a postcard from each new place you visit. On that postcard write down one of your favorite moments from your trip and keep your postcards in a scrapbook, or in a special memory box, for you to look at in the future.

Our Trail Adventures

Trail Names
Dad: Pack Mule
Mom: Granola Gal
Noah: Trail Blitzer
Tessa: Baby Foxy

Favorite Hikes
Dad: Bettmerhorn to Bettmersee
Mom: Obersteinberg
Noah: Globi Trail
Tessa: Cardada to Cimetta

Favorite Snack on the Trail
Dad: Ice Cream
Mom: Apples and salty nuts
Noah: Cheesy Crackers
Tessa: Chocolate

Favorite Post Hike Meal
Dad: Rösti
Mom: Rösti and Apple Cake
Noah: Chicken Nuggets with French Fries
Tessa: Sausage

Total kilometers hiked in 2018
390+

Favorite Overnight Stay
Dad: Berghaus Bort, Grindelwald
Mom: Appenzell, Berggasthaus Forelle am Seealpsee
Noah: Hotel Restaurant Les Etagnes, Nendaz
Tessa: Berghotel Tgantieni, Lenzerheide

Favorite Area of the Swiss Alps
Dad: UNESCO Swiss Alps Jungfrau-Aletsch World Heritage Area
Mom: Berner Oberland
Noah: Lenzerheide
Tessa: Ticino

Coolest Trail Find
Dad: Peverelli's Bakery in Bellinzona
Mom: Alpine newts at the end of the Panorama Trail in Nendaz
Noah: Fossils in Frick
Tessa: Crystals at the Anenhütte

Best Playground
Dad: Berghaus Bort
Mom: Mürren Flower Park
Noah: Tgantieni
Tessa: Nendaz

Favorite Theme Trail
Dad: Muggestutz
Mom: Cardada Scavenger Hunt
Noah: Globi Trail – Lenzerheide
Tessa: Globi Trail – Lenzerheide

Favorite Animal Discovered While Hiking
Dad: Ibex
Mom: The tiny frogs on the trail of the Bisse de Saxon
Noah: Sämi the Butterfly
Tessa: Salamanders

Funniest Moment
Dad: The automatic ice cream machine in Wasserauen
Mom: Hands down, when Noah threw his hiking shoe on the roof of a hotel
Noah: Riding the zip-line at the Les Paccots playground
Tessa: Having a butterfly land on me

Favorite Memory While Hiking
Dad: Experiencing one of the largest caves in Switzerland, the Vallorbe Caves
Mom: When our daughter picked up trash out of a river and said, "Mom, look at this sad pollution someone left in the river." It made me realize that she is aware that the trash was not in the proper location and that she cared enough to scoop the trash out of the river.
Noah: Playing in the Lido in Lenzerheide and at the huge marble run in Lenzerheide
Tessa: Seeing alpine newts in the lake in Nendaz

Hello Fresh Air Kids!

Don't forget to take the *Fresh Air Kids Switzerland – My Book of Discoveries* with you each time you head outside. This activity book was designed to help you keep track of and remember all of your hikes. We have also included coloring pages, special challenges, and scavenger hunts, which will make your next outdoor experience a memorable one. Happy adventures!

**Fresh Air Kids Switzerland –
My Book of Discoveries**
Melinda & Robert Schoutens
ISBN: 978-2-940481-65-1

Fresh Air Kids Switzerland
52 Inspiring Hikes That Will Make Kids and Parents Happy
ISBN: 978-2-940481-62-0

Graphic Design and Illustrations: Felix Kindelán
Photos: Melinda and Robert Schoutens
Proofreading: Alasdair Cullen, Aaron Melick
Printed in the Czech Republic

www.helvetiq.com